Love Side Up

Ernest Randolph

Published by Ernest Randolph, 2024.

While every precaution has been taken in the preparation of this book, the publisher assumes no responsibility for errors or omissions, or for damages resulting from the use of the information contained herein.

LOVE SIDE UP

First edition. October 1, 2024.

Copyright © 2024 Ernest Randolph.

ISBN: 979-8991368001

Written by Ernest Randolph.

Table of Contents

PART 1: THE SOURCE OF A GOOD LIFE 1
Chapter 1: The Troubles of Life 3
Chapter 2: The Winemaker 13
Chapter 3: Jesus Saves 21
Chapter 4: Ain't Nothin' Like the Real Jesus 27
Chapter 5: Is He the One? 35
Chapter 6: Jesus is the Source of a Good Life 41
APPENDIX to Part 1: The Fate of Those Who Don't Follow Jesus 49
PART 2: THE JOURNEY TO A GOOD LIFE 59
Chapter 7: Using the Right Fuel 63
Chapter 8: Getting on the Right Road 73
Chapter 9: Starting with the Essentials 81
Chapter 10: The Navigator 93
Chapter 11: Turn at the Cross 101
Chapter 12: Worthy to Travel 111
Chapter 13: A New Way 117
Chapter 14: Why Not Take the Old Way? 123
Chapter 15: Breaking Down 131
Chapter 16: Needed Repairs 139
Chapter 17: Miraculously Fixed 151
Chapter 18: Routine Maintenance 157
Chapter 19: Backing Up When We Make a Wrong Turn 165
PART 3: ARRIVING AT A GOOD LIFE 173
Chapter 20: A Good Life for the Least of These 175
Chapter 21: Why Does a Good Life Include Suffering? 183
Chapter 22: Love Is the Key 191
Chapter 23: Living A Good Life 201
Chapter 24: Things Not Included 205
Chapter 25: Love-Side-Up 213
ENDNOTES 227

PART 1: THE SOURCE OF A GOOD LIFE

Chapter 1: The Troubles of Life

And now these three remain: faith, hope, and love. But the greatest of these is love.

I Corinthians 13:13 (NIV)

THE NECESSITY FOR LOVE is the most fundamental need of every human being. Without it, one will face a life lacking meaning and purpose, and their existence can spiral to destruction. When a soul falls into a dark state of mind where they believe they are loved by no one, it seems impossible for them to perceive or achieve recognizable value and worth. Sadly, throughout the millennia of human history there have been countless numbers of people who have experienced this travesty of a loveless existence. Too many people have lived horrible, or at least not-so-special lives—all alone and struggling to understand why they were important. They exist without knowing genuine love, making their search for meaning almost impossible to attain.

When I was much younger, I witnessed just such a tragedy in the life of my classmate, Mikey. He lived in a poor, chaotic household with his three troubled sisters and his single mother who was overbearing, uneducated, and very much on the wild side. His only father figure was her occasional irreputable boyfriends. It seemed everything was stacked against him from the start.

I first met Mikey when my mother rented a small house in our backyard to his family. In a spot between their house and mine, I had meticulously fashioned a Matchbox car kingdom with tunnels, buildings, and roads, of which I was very proud. Not knowing how much it meant to me, Mikey managed to destroy the entire creation in minutes. My anger was such that I refused to talk to him for the three months they lived there.

I ran into Mikey again in sixth grade. We went to the same school and it was apparent that he had no friends. He dressed in old dirty clothes, usually had smudges on his face, and wore a no-style crew haircut.

Although Mikey had it hard, sixth grade was also a challenging year for me. I was starting at a new school, struggling to make friends, and dealing with my mother having a new man in her life. I was enduring the worst year I can remember as a child.

Mikey wanted to be friends but if I agreed to associate with him that would end any chance of me being liked by others. Also, since we didn't like each other that much, I had no reason to risk him destroying my kingdom as he did when we were kids. Sadly, I did not know how badly Mikey was hurting inside. It was less than a year later that he took his own life. Me preserving the friendships I had built was not worth it; the other kids ended up hating me regardless of what I did.

Mikey's life was not good. He felt alone and hopeless in his horrible circumstances and decided that suicide was the only way out. Many children are overwhelmed even when they have adults to rescue them. It's not just children who are underwater; at any age people can experience their lives crashing down around them. One can feel they cannot bear the consequences of what they have broken or what others have destroyed. At any given moment, the pleasures of life can be so great that one's world is filled with happiness and smiles, yet at less fortunate times, their situation may make them uncomfortable or worse, and one can find themselves drowning in agony. At that point, a *good life* seems entirely unattainable.

The trouble and suffering that threatens the quality of our lives can come from multiple sources. We are deeply hurt when we experience the loss of a relationship and distraught when we face money problems. Outside pressures, inner turmoil, and family disputes seem to bring unwelcome torment to us all. Natural disasters, sickness, and death fill us with unavoidable and unexpected misery from which we cannot hide. We may be discouraged because we are not where we want to be. Perhaps we have not met our goals or, worse, lost what we care about deeply. These events are unexpected individual trials that are unique to each of us. Some people may even have overwhelming fears of unavoidable common things like getting sick, injured, or personally rejected. These fears can result in phobias which can lead to an inability to go outside, or they may keep us from having the courage to talk to a stranger. Struggle and even suffering are an integral part of being human. We are loaded with turmoil as we navigate this life.

While our burdens can come from multiple directions and with different intensities, they can also be self-created. I have seen people allow themselves to suffer tremendously because the painter painted their room a slightly darker shade of the right color. The fret over a scratch on a new vehicle can change our demeanor toward those we love. We suffer because our steak is medium, not medium-rare, because someone took our parking spot, or because a driver takes a second longer at the light than we judge necessary. I am not making light of suffering but merely pointing out that some of our sufferings are a matter of perspective. What an individual considers to be the cause of suffering can be hard to nail down.

Our life structure, the personal kingdom we build, consists of our value system and the people we associate with. It's common to believe that getting these things right is the key to having a *good life*. The cause of our duress, whatever the reason, can put us in a state of desperation and angst because we are not living at the level we want to live.

Often, we self-inflict our torment because we obsess about fulfilling our desire to improve our life circumstances in pursuit of a *good life*. In our quest, we find it can take intense work to measure up to the demands we put on ourselves. Even worse, the more success we achieve, the more pressure we place on others in our lives to perform to the level of our success. As our circumstances become more favorable, we may see ourselves as superior to those who don't meet our new standards. When our best efforts fail to meet the expectations we have created for ourselves, we might blame it on others and may abandon our current life in search of one that is more fulfilling.

Finding ways to solve our problems and achieve our aspirations starts from the moment we are born. As young children, we look for ways to minimize our distress or to avoid it altogether as we build our personal kingdoms. Hopefully, we learn to trust and respond appropriately to the people around us. Our parents are the first people we trust to improve our lives, and they seem to respond to every need. We may agree to add a brother, a sister, an extended family member, a babysitter, or even a friendly stranger to our trusted few. All who enter must be approved by us. We cry at the ones we don't like and smile at the ones we do. If severe neglect or a traumatic experience happens to us early on in our lives, it can have a lasting negative effect on how we give and receive love, and it can damage our ability to cope with life's future problems.

As we grow and form an ethical value system, we face new challenges. The world becomes no longer just about us. Our power to disrupt and control people's lives begins to fade quickly, tables turn, and we are corrected or ignored when we are mean or demanding. We are disciplined when we hurt someone or when we scream because we don't get everything we want. Some people even decide they don't like us. The building of our kingdom gets exponentially more complicated with each passing day.

As we enter school, we learn kingdom building is highly competitive, with a horde of other kids on the same journey. In America we are told if we participate in the competition and do everything right, we can become anything we want, maybe even the president. This proposal can overwhelm us with an urgency to decide what we must learn and who we must become to achieve our desired kingdom and stay ahead of our competition.

Transitioning to adulthood, we face the difficult question of higher education. More significant learning is expensive and challenging. We must be convinced it will be a beneficial building block.

The prospect of obtaining a spouse, a life partner to join us on this journey, weighs heavily on our hearts. The desire for companionship and the wish for someone permanent to give and receive love can be exciting and daunting at the same time. Our hope for a spouse may come with a longing to have children and build a family much like the family of our youth—improved of course.

Because kingdom building is complex, we must seek and receive help along the way. Think again of your mother. Her arms are the safest and first place we shelter from suffering. She is the satisfaction of our hunger and the consoler of our emotional needs. But Mom is limited and fallible and will only be sufficient for a while, if at all. What about Dad? He seems to put his head down, drive forward, and take on life to build his kingdom. He is the perceived leader who protects, provides, corrects, and comforts. Can he show us how to cope with our trials and tribulations? Sometimes, but fathers also make mistakes and often fail to live up to our expectations.

As we mature into young adults, parents help less and even start contributing to our life pressures. They expect a level of performance from us and are only sometimes there when we need them. A few of their ideas and actions are even destructive. To craft our kingdoms, we must move on with our lives without them sheltering and protecting us. If we do not learn to grow from our struggles and to keep moving forward, our struggles could grow more prominent, overtake us, and leave us with no ability to cope with difficulties. If we are going to build a *good life* on our own, we should use the wisdom our parents give us, yet it is not that simple, we also must be given the freedom to experience the truth of how it applies to our lives in success or failure.

As we get older, we may find that our internal weaknesses may be the biggest hindrances to discovering a *good life*. Our motives can be conflicted, and our initiatives fail to get off the ground. We may seem to have it all together, but what is happening inside us? Multitudes of inner complications can derail even the most straightforward plans. We may experience disappointment, loneliness, depression, anger, angst, boredom, and regret, often not even knowing why. When we are at our worst, our hearts can contain a whole labyrinth of negative emotions and thoughts that block our success.

We all are on a journey to build our kingdom, attempting to obtain a comfortable and *good life*. Our challenge is to find ways to lessen or prevent our struggle and to reduce our suffering. Our answers, despite our best attempts, are not guaranteed. Our solutions can sometimes be wrong and bring worse results, or we may experience others sabotaging our attempts to improve. At times, our plans come crashing down at different stages for reasons out of our control. When our plans fail, our aspirations are not always scuttled; initial ideas can be salvaged, corrected, and rebuilt. In the process, our vision of what brings a *good life* can become disillusioned. It may be in a moment of despair that we become aware that we alone are not enough, and at that juncture, we find ourselves in want of a higher power. At such pivotal moments, we decide if seeking a higher power will help bring about a *good life*.

When considering a belief in God, many are troubled by the problem of evil. Outside threats like disease, death, corruption, sabotage, and natural disasters affect us all. Evil appears to run its course in this world, whether caused by humans, a supernatural force, or nature. Since evil and chaos exist, then some are quick to assume a good God does not exist because they see evil and chaos as things a good God would do something about. Or, if God exists as an all-powerful being, and He does not—from our perspective—choose to intervene, God Himself is then either evil or impotent for allowing the evil. This train of thought causes many to see God as participating in or orchestrating evil if He oversees all circumstances and is truly Sovereign. While there is no simple answer, it is more complex than questioning God's existence or blaming Him for evil. The presence of great evils does not necessarily preclude the existence of good and powerful God or show Him to be evil. Our lack of knowledge of how events fit the overall scheme substantially limits our ability to make those judgments. His ways are far beyond our simple, finite minds but it is essential to understand evil's necessity if we want to include the idea of God in our kingdom.

For the God of the Bible, the idea of free will is the primary way to explain and understand the existence evil. If humans are free agents with the ability to choose to seek God or reject Him, then evil must and does exist. Indirectly, God created the possibility of evil and foresaw the horrible consequences that would come because of entities rejecting Him. It appears He decided that the creation of distinct volitional persons was worth allowing imminent evil and destruction—it was worth the real love, true justice, imaginative creativity, and friendship, all coming from persons who could choose independently of His will. Despite evil in this world, I see the overall goodness in God's plan of creating free agents as almost incomprehensibly brilliant. God allowed people to reject Him because He desired to create a people who could and would voluntarily choose to love Him. The freedom to choose allows for true love and makes relationships meaningful and authentic. This choice to love Him necessitated the ability to decide not to receive God's love.

When the first humans chose against God's love, they opened the door for evil to enter the world.

Looking at the account of Adam and Eve, along with early biblical history, informs us about the beginning of evil in this world as humans rejected God and set out on a quest to solve their problems by building their kingdoms without God. When God created us, we had it easy in the garden before the Fall, but existence was not without work or struggle. Have you ever considered how difficult it would be to name thousands of animals? What about tending a large orchard? Adam and Eve had plenty of work and struggle in the garden as they lived in a relationship with God, growing in love and truth.

Unfortunately, Adam and Eve chose to face their struggle without God guiding them. Instead, they sought the "knowledge of good and evil." (Gen. 2:17, NASB) Their rebellious decision led to struggle, suffering, and eventually death. The first humans gave up their paradise because they were tricked into thinking there was a better way. They attempted to achieve a *good life* according to their making, a kingdom without God's rule. That journey would take humanity to some very dark places. (Although Adam and Eve had the choice to not seek knowledge on their own, true freedom demanded they have that opportunity. It's interesting to observe, that for some of us, if we do not know evil and its consequences, it is not easy for us to see the greatness of God's goodness and grace. Many cannot be resolute in the conviction that they will never turn from God without knowing the wrong way.)

After the fall, Adam and Eve's son Cain chose to grow crops, which God had prescribed man to do in the curse. God said that man would toil and struggle to bring fruit from the ground because of his rebellion (Gen. 3:17-19). Cain succeeded in reducing his struggles and increasing his comfort with his crop. He brought his harvest to God with pride in what he had achieved. His brother Abel came to God in humility, willing to sacrifice the resource that brought him comfort. Abel gave an item of great value, professing that God—not the work of his hands—is the source of our life and our provider. In his pride, Cain declared that he had overcome the struggle God placed on him, overcoming God's curse. This did not please God. Abel, on the other hand, was accepted by God. In humility, he copied God's example of how his sins were covered and how he was to be made acceptable in God's sight by sacrificing an animal. It was then that Cain murdered Abel over his frustration with God rejecting him (Gen. 4:2-10). This is the earliest account of someone dealing with struggle and guilt completely wrong by blaming another for their problems in life. His act set the stage for the future of humanity.

Humans became exceedingly wicked in their quest to build a *good life*––willing to abuse others and abandon God. The complete freedom God gave mankind did not result in the intended relationship God wanted with us. Instead, it resulted in horrible hate and destruction, which had to be dealt with. God caused a great flood to destroy His creation and all of humanity except Noah and his family.

Humans entered a new era after the flood, yet we were still not ready to give up the struggle for a *good life* through the knowledge of good and evil. Mercifully, God chose to participate in our quest to overcome evil and struggle. He gave us an early covenant at the time of Noah, and He later gave the law through Moses to teach us how to love, do good, and avoid evil. This was probably to His regret because, as illustrated in the case of Cain, God knew people would depend more on the laws for salvation than they would on Him. He foresaw laws would be a barrier to a loving relationship, yet He gave humans the law because they could not restrain their ability to cause great suffering without it.

When humanity rejects God's plan, they quickly find themselves using or sacrificing the lives of other human beings for their pleasure and comfort, and to reduce their suffering. They may practice slavery, abortion, and murder. They may instigate wars and other evils to achieve a better future. Humanity has often justified evil actions based on a human understanding of good and evil. It seems there is no end to what people are willing to do to others to keep their own comfort and power. They rebel against God while building their kingdom, trying to demonstrate that they can achieve a *good life* without Him.

When humans walked away from God, they walked away from the source of life and entered a life of trouble. They walked away from a relationship with their father, friend, and teacher. They walked away from the one who loved them and desired an everlasting, deep, and meaningful relationship with them. God wanted them back and sought to help them in their suffering, but relationships require participation on both sides. It is disastrous when humans build their kingdoms at great expense to themselves and others. God wants to answer our troubles when he is invited into our kingdom, especially as something more than merely a rule-giver who we must appease. Jesus said: "In this world you will have trouble. But take heart! I have overcome the world" (John 16:33, NIV).

Chapter 2: The Winemaker

"They have no wine."

John 2:3 (NKJV)

ALTHOUGH MOST OF US live as if we have our lives under control, we are often desperate to find ways to improve our circumstances. We desire answers to explain the emptiness we feel on the inside, and we fail to understand why things don't work out the way we want them to on the outside.

How do we measure a good, full, and well-lived life? How do we know we are getting life right? These are difficult questions to answer, even if we believe life is a great and precious gift given by God. It is even harder when our life circumstances are unbearable or we feel life is empty and unfair, and we are unknown and misunderstood.

One way to look at our quest for a vibrant existence is to compare the source of a *good life* to wine in a bottle. The following fictional story illustrates that comparison.

> Stan was a somewhat average young man from an ordinary family and with no unusual problems, still he felt as though he had been born with a deficit of wine. Other people appeared to get more generous portions and better wine early on in life, while all he saw was his small, half-empty bottle. He panicked as he started using his wine, fearing it would run out. Stan found ways to replenish his supply through hard work, education, kind deeds, and

religious practices, but always seemed to come up short. He assessed his bottle only to find the level as low as ever.

Stan wondered if someone else could fill his bottle. He sought friends who would share their wine with him, but they also wanted a large portion of his. As they took too much, he would beg them to stop, but it was no use. They eventually left him completely dry. Fleeing for his life, he found himself alone and empty yet again.

Then the unthinkable happened to a girl Stan knew. Some people took her bottle, abused her wine, and left her empty and broken beyond repair. They tricked her with a false promise of an abundance of wine. Sadly, she fell for their ruse and was left with nothing to carry her wine in. She could not bear the thought that her only source of wine was to pass from person to person, begging for a few drops. Seeing no way forward, she ended her beautiful life.

As a result of this tragedy, Stan realized he needed to find someone who would love and cherish his wine, or else he might end up like his friend. Then it happened; he fell in love. He finally found a loving soul to give his wine to, and she intended to share hers with him. They committed to caring for one another's wine as long as they both would live.

After some years, the relationship faltered. They didn't give to one another as Stan had envisioned. He tried to share as much wine as possible, but she seemed to share very little. Maybe she saw it the opposite way, but Stan felt betrayed, cracked, and empty. He was running out of wine, and she would only share a dribble—leaving him barely enough to survive. He then discovered his companion was sharing her wine with another and not even a drop was left for him.

Feeling hopeless and empty, Stan left the relationship but was not unscathed. His bottle had developed additional cracks from the hurt and betrayal, which left him incredibly low on wine. He desperately needed to find a solution. In his despair, he tried alcohol, drugs, and selfish living to cope. These solutions filled the bottle with a substitute wine, diluting and damaging the small amount of good wine left.

Stan then turned in a darker direction to find more wine. He was not proud of some of the things he did. He hurt others and stole their wine. His ugly behavior seemed to bring only wine that soured quickly, and it added little, if any good wine to his bottle. To justify his behavior, he told himself: "He wasn't so bad, everyone must live, and he'd taken from others as they'd taken from him."

As Stan looked at his life, he realized how awful he was behaving towards others through selfish actions which damaged the very vulnerable. He wanted to change and was determined to give others more than he took, believing it might make up for some of his wrongs.

He found if he was careful, loving, and kind, others would willingly share wine with him. He sought to befriend the right people while he worked, strived, meditated, exercised, laughed, and played to bring positive growth to his life. Stan even found an intimate relationship that met his need for connection as a person. It seemed to be working, except Stan still ran into takers and thieves. Moreover, when he was honest with himself, he knew deep down he was still forced to selfishly take what he needed to survive at the expense of others.

No matter what Stan did, his actions weren't enough to fix the leaks from his past. In his desperation, he went to a counselor. She showed him how to plug some holes, which helped somewhat.

Outwardly, it appeared all was well, but on the inside, his bottle was still cracked and empty.

Then, he met a unique new friend. This friend shared an abundance of good wine with him and told Stan to come back if he needed more. He suspiciously thought: "Where has he acquired this wine?" When his friend told him it was from the supernatural "Maker of Wine," Stan guessed that he might be a little crazy. The friend went on to explain that Stan's empty and cracked bottle was not only the result of the foolish things Stan had done, but also what others had done to him. He also explained that everyone was born with cracks, and humans have no choice but to steal each other's wine. This didn't sit well with Stan. How could this person know so much about him and what he had done?

Stan continued to fume to himself: "His bottle was fine except for a few cracks. His new friend had been going to this winemaker since he was young, he didn't know all the other ways to fill and fix one's bottle. It's silly that my new friend thinks this winemaker is the only source." He fled the idea and searched for another way to fill and fix his bottle—to no avail. No other wine was like the wine his friend said came from the Maker of Wine.

Finally, Stan agreed to meet this so-called winemaker but made no promises. The Maker of Wine kindly offered Stan wine and said it would never run out. Stan sensed that this was the answer to his cracked, empty bottle. He cried out: "Please give me this wine!" The Maker of Wine motioned that he needed to see Stan's bottle.

Trembling, Stan feared the winemaker might be like all the rest and take more wine than he could afford to give. Upon seeing the winemaker's tender and loving demeanor, he slowly began to show his bottle to him.

The Maker of Wine proclaimed softly: "I can't put my wine in that old, cracked bottle." He motioned for Stan to hand it over.

"Stop, wait, would he give it back?" Stan feared. He had never completely let go of his bottle. Remembering what happened to the young girl who let go of hers, it didn't work out so well! But the Maker's expression was gentle, and his new friend had told him many great things about this Maker of Wine.

Stan cautiously gave up his bottle. He trusted the Maker to fix his flawed vessel, refill it, and return it. The Maker of Wine did not do as he expected, he did something much better. The Maker of Wine gave him a new bottle that was already full and would never run dry.

The allegory about Stan illustrates the transforming power of Jesus in someone's life. Jesus is the giver of the incredible lifesaving gift humanity desperately needs. A loving relationship with Jesus brings new freedom and empowerment that can fill us beyond measure as He grows our love for Him, others, and ourselves. Jesus is the true answer that transforms our lives in a deeply meaningful way, far exceeding our expectations. He fills us with eternal new wine, renewing our forever relationship with Him. He enters us and becomes a part of our kingdom.

Tragically, like the girl in the story, sometimes people fail to overcome their troubles. Unfortunately, their situation can seem beyond repair, even when they know Jesus. It happened to Mikey, and sadly, I could not show him the love of Jesus.

Humanity's loss of a relationship with the giver of life resulted in a loss of our true meaning and purpose of existence. It created a situation where we must do whatever it takes to ensure our value and build our kingdom without God. While scraping out value and purpose from less-than-ideal sources, our actions can become a form of slavery to our worthlessness, forcing us to practice selfish and sometimes hurtful behavior to achieve and warrant our significance.

I cannot accept this lack of universal significance and have no reason to. It is more likely and more viable to believe the supernatural God can provide the answer for everyone to have great significance despite their achievements. Jesus' creation of us, love for us, and sacrifice for us imparts to us true importance and meaning.

In contrast to following Jesus, human solutions to affect the *good life* are primarily performed in our own strength. At some point in our efforts, we will land on a spectrum of pride versus wretchedness. In facing our struggle, do we overcome it and succeed, resulting in pride, or do we succumb to its overwhelming pressure, fail in the world's eyes, our family's eyes, or even our own eyes, and become wretched? We often are not entirely one way or the other. Sometimes, we feel proud of what we have overcome, and moments later, we feel wretched about our shortcomings. Both states—pride and wretchedness—affect how we treat ourselves and others around us. Our greatest efforts can cause more internal suffering, leaving us asking: "What is the answer?"

French mathematician and philosopher Blaise Pascal wrote that Jesus is the only simultaneous answer to our wretchedness and our pride.[1] The wretched either believe themselves unworthy or are so proud of their wretchedness that they will not admit they need saving. The proud have trouble humbling themselves because of their pride in their self-sufficiency. In this pride, they cannot recognize they are wrong and admit they are hurting inside. Through Christ's death, the wretched are lifted up, and the high are made low, for we are all sinners in need of a savior. We come to Christ realizing that in our deficiency, we need and want a relationship with Him. Our life with God starts when we acknowledge our sins and brokenness, receive His forgiveness, and decide to put our trust in Him. The Spirit changes our lives, whether by lowering our pride or by lifting our self-worth.

Our decision to follow Jesus will not instantly fix the mess we find ourselves in. However, discovering your heavenly purpose—to be in an intimate relationship with the creator God through Jesus Christ, in fellowship with the Spirit—will get you on the right road. Being aware of our failures and accepting the great value Jesus bestows upon us is hard, but when we are reconciled to God and get our heavenly purpose right, it is the first step on the journey to a *good life* and the first step to discovering our earthly purpose. A reconciled relationship with God is the foundational cornerstone of a healthy, truthful, and loving life; it is the source and fulfillment of our purpose and meaning.

When we follow Jesus and find our purpose and value from a relationship with Him, we are no longer left beholden to the value we give ourselves and the value others may provide us with. We then enter a relationship where our value comes from God's love being lavished upon us because we are the children of the Father. For Christians, the love of God is not a vague, peaceful feeling; it is profoundly personal and begins to address our most pressing concerns. We start on the path of learning and believing the teachings of Jesus, following Him as a disciple, and being filled with His Spirit. We then begin to realize the blessings of existing as one of God's children, and we begin to experience an internal transformation with Jesus walking with us through our struggles. The closer we come to fully know and experience the truth of what Jesus did for us, and the more we fellowship with His Spirit, the more Jesus will grow us in truth and love, even as we pass through our life's greatest successes and biggest dilemmas. The more we grow, the more we will experience God's love, which is the answer to what is truly missing in our lives.

Chapter 3: Jesus Saves

And there is salvation in no one else, for there is no other name under heaven given among people by which we must be saved.

Acts 4:12 (NET)

IT HAS BEEN OVER FIFTY years since I knelt with my mother at a Child Evangelism Fellowship Club and accepted Christ as my Savior. I prayed the sinner's prayer and asked Jesus into my heart that day. It seemed simple enough, but my understanding of Christianity proceeded to get more complicated from there. Was I saved? Was it real? Should I do it again? In junior high, I wasn't sure I wanted to be a Christian. As a senior in high school, I wrote a tremendously complicated paper on salvation inspired by books found in my family library. It was long and cumbersome because I had trouble saying what I needed to say in a few short words. I also wondered if I needed the baptism of the Holy Spirit to be saved and to experience God fully. I pounded my pastor with all my hard spiritual questions during Sunday school. He became so frustrated with having to answer them right before his sermon that he quickly found someone else to teach the class. I needed help finding answers, so I headed off to a Christian college.

My understanding of the Christian life has come a long way since then. Not that I am through learning, but I have a sufficient understanding of the big picture. Even still, when I read the Bible, some things are clear, some are deep, some take scholarly study, some are mysterious, and some things I still do not understand. I ask God, "Why didn't You put this in simple instructions: step one, step two, step three?" Then, I remember, "Oh yeah, we fail to read and pay attention to simple instructions." Human minds are so complicated that simple instructions bore us—yet we complain about complex directions.

During my undergraduate studies, I attended college with Greg Stier, a gifted evangelist from Dare to Share Ministries. He constantly told me how straightforward sharing the gospel was. In his free time, Greg would ask perfect strangers if they knew where they were going when they died. I found it hard to approach the gospel in such a direct manner. I did not understand the gospel as easily as Greg did, and unfortunately, I avoided evangelizing with him.

Several years later, I ran into Greg when I took my youth group to a Dare to Share event. After the presentation, half of them went to the front of the room and publicly accepted Christ. I had worked with these youths for over a year and tried to present Christianity as a simple choice in my talks, but very few publicly accepted Christ after I spoke. Why didn't they choose to follow Jesus when I explained the gospel? Perhaps I made it too complicated or assumed they were already believers. God has more to do with it than Greg or myself, but what was my part? Youth groups often discuss issues that can muddy the waters when dealt with apart from the gospel. My group needed to hear the simple message that Jesus loves them, forgives them, has a destiny for their lives, and all they had to do was decide to believe and follow Him.

When I was twenty, my ten-year-old niece asked me, "How does someone become a Christian?" After two years of studying to be a youth pastor, I still had trouble answering that question. It did not help that my brother, whose beliefs differed from mine, was sitting at the table with us. I got so wrapped up in explaining the issues surrounding salvation I skipped over the simple answer, and, not surprisingly, her interest faded.

Paul gave the simple answer to the Philippian jailer. The story of his gospel presentation is found in the book of Acts:

> About midnight Paul and Silas were praying and singing hymns to God, and the other prisoners were listening to them. Suddenly there was such a violent earthquake that the foundations of the prison were shaken. At once all the prison doors flew open, and everyone's chains came loose. The jailer woke up, and when he saw the prison doors open, he drew his sword and was about to kill

himself because he thought the prisoners had escaped. But Paul shouted, "Don't harm yourself! We are all here!" The jailer called for lights, rushed in and fell trembling before Paul and Silas. He then brought them out and asked, "Sirs, what must I do to be saved?" They replied, "Believe in the Lord Jesus, and you will be saved—you and your household."

Acts 16:25–31 (NIV)

This was such a dramatic day and night in the life of a first-century Philippian jailer. He was tasked with guarding these Jewish troublemakers who would not stop praying and singing—even after they were beaten. Then, an earthquake leading to a possible prison escape occurred, and the only honorable thing left to do was to end his own life. which might save his family from shame and destruction. Yet, he sensed something supernatural when Paul and Silas acted in kindness and love towards him by not leaving when the gates were opened. The guard wanted what they had and exclaimed: "Sirs, what must I do to be saved?" His life was disrupted, and he was drawn in by what he had seen, heard, and felt. This feeling and observation was so strong that it created a desire in him to turn to a new foreign God for his salvation. His god and government required his death for him and his family, and Jesus offered new life. To his question Paul replied: "Believe in the Lord Jesus, and you will be saved—you and your household."

The jailor had built his kingdom by creating a way of life for himself, which had worked up to this point. It took an earthquake and a potential prison break to bring him to where he realized his plan was insufficient. This event is the type of dramatic conversion that people are easily impressed with. Although God does use significant events sometimes, I think He is more impressed with a simple, humble decision by someone to love Him without fanfare. There are many reasons an individual may turn from their current assumptions and believe in Jesus for their salvation. I think God is equally happy, no matter the reason.

Some Christians, including myself, make the gospel message complicated. The gospel is as simple as Paul proclaimed: "Believe in the Lord Jesus, and you will be saved." A child can understand it, but adults seem to struggle. I make it difficult because I want to know the whole picture. Sometimes, I can be a slow learner with a thick skull. How can this be so hard? Why didn't I share a simple gospel message so long ago when my niece asked me about salvation? Instead, I made the conversation about convincing another person to believe. Sharing the gospel is the simple task of presenting others with the choice to believe in Jesus.

The simple gospel is the good news about a relationship with God made possible through Jesus and His work on the cross. The apostle Paul clearly stated the path to salvation in his recorded reply to the Philippian jailer when he said, "Believe in the Lord Jesus, and you will be saved" (Acts 16:31, NIV). It took me forty years to be convinced Paul's simple statement summed up the whole gospel.

The simple gospel is expressed to us in Scripture as a simple choice to believe in Jesus and enter into a relationship with Him.

> For with the heart one believes and thus has righteousness and with the mouth one confesses and thus has salvation.
>
> Romans 10:10 (NET)

Salvation is the result of our belief in Jesus. When we believe, we are saved.

> I tell you the solemn truth, the one who hears my message and believes the one who sent me has eternal life and will not be condemned, but has crossed over from death to life.
>
> John 5:24 (NET)

Sometimes, I wish I had a do-over button, considering all the mistakes I have made. God did give us all a do-over button in the work of Christ on the cross. We do not have to fall on a sword to fix the mess we made; all we must do is believe to be saved. A simple decision to believe changes our entire lives, now and for eternity. When we enter a relationship with God, it is similar to any relationship. It takes work and gets messy at times, but the relationship is more than worth it. Although this book summarizes how our relationship with God is lived out, these are not step-by-step instructions. There is no system of knowing if we are doing it exactly right. We need to work "right" out on our journey with Jesus as he builds His kingdom in our lives, with Himself as the king.

Chapter 4: Ain't Nothin' Like the Real Jesus

He said to them, "But who do you say that I am?" Simon Peter answered, "You are the Christ, the Son of the living God."

Matthew 16:15–16 (NET)

WHAT DOES IT TAKE TO believe that Jesus was the savior of the world, God in the flesh? The Philippian jailor was able to believe in Jesus based on the actions and words of Paul and Silas. For many, to make a decision of this magnitude requires a deeper understanding of who Jesus is.

It would help to know what Jesus claimed about His identity and why He deserves our attention. The quintessential claim He made was that He was God in the flesh, i.e., the creator of the universe. He made this proclamation on several occasions, saying openly, "The Father and I are one" (John 10:30, NET). His claim of deity is most clearly shown in the discourse recorded in John 8, in which Jesus declared, "Before Abraham came into existence, I AM" (John 8:58, NET). He claimed the name of God, which Moses had recorded when the Lord spoke to him from the burning bush (Exod. 3:14). We are assured this statement was recognized as a claim to be God because the Jews picked up stones to kill Him for blasphemy.

John, one of Jesus' disciples and closest friends, wrote eloquently about who Jesus is, calling Him the Word and the light:

> In the beginning was the Word, and the Word was with God, and the Word was God. He was with God in the beginning. Through him all things were made; without him nothing was made that has been made. In him was life, and that life was the light of all

mankind. The light shines in the darkness, and the darkness has not overcome it. ...The true light that gives light to everyone was coming into the world. ...The Word became flesh and made his dwelling among us. We have seen his glory, the glory of the one and only Son, who came from the Father, full of grace and truth.

John 1:1–5, 9, 14 (NIV)

The Bible goes on to say much more about who Jesus is. He was and is God, the king of glory (Ps. 24:9), the great I Am (Isa. 48:12), the creator of the universe (John 1:3), the beginning and the end (Rev. 22:13), the source of all knowledge (Proverbs 9:10), energy, and strength (1 Chron. 29:12). the source of the very existence of life itself (John 1:4), the author of our being (Gen. 1:26, Ps. 139:13), giver of our consciousness (Gen. 2:7), and the one whose face Moses could not even look at (Exod. 13:18–20). Even though the disciples believed Jesus was the Messiah sent from God, I am not sure they fully comprehended Jesus was the all-powerful creator God until after He rose from the dead.

Jesus is not only mentioned in the Bible but outside the Bible as well. Josephus, a first-century Jewish historian, wrote of Him:

> At this time there was a wise man who was called Jesus. And his conduct was good, and [he] was known to be virtuous. And many people from among the Jews and the other nations became his disciples. Pilate condemned him to be crucified and to die. And those who had become his disciples did not abandon his discipleship. They reported that he had appeared to them three days after his crucifixion and that he was alive. Accordingly, he was perhaps the Messiah concerning whom the prophets have recounted wonders.[2]

Roman documents also mention Jesus. In chronicling the burning of Rome in 64 A.D., Tacitus mentions that Emperor Nero falsely blamed "the persons commonly called Christians, who were hated for their enormities.

Christus, the founder of the name, was put to death by Pontius Pilate, procurator of Judea in the reign of Tiberius.[3]

Shortly before Tacitus penned his mention of Jesus, Roman governor Pliny the Younger wrote to Emperor Trajan that early Christians would "sing hymns to Christ as to a god."[4]

Jesus is even mentioned in the Talmud, which are Jewish historical records of events that they thought worthy to preserve over the centuries. Parts of the Babylonian/Munich Talmud are thought to be contemporary to the time of Christ. It contains a record of a figure who was hung and not stoned for deceiving the people with sorcery. It reads:

> It was taught: On the Eve of Passover they hung accurate, the accurate. And the herald went out before him for forty days [saying]: 'Yeshu the Notzri [Jesus of Nazareth] will go out to be stoned for sorcery and misleading and enticing Israel [to idolatry]. Any who knows [anything] in his defense must come and declare concerning him.' But no one came to his defense so they hung him on the Eve of Passover.[5]

This passage contains a close rendition of His name, "Yeshu the Notzri," almost definitely meaning Jesus of Nazareth. Hearing the name, "accurate, the accurate," brings the clear reminder of what Jesus continually claimed when He spoke: "I tell you the truth." Claiming that He was doing "sorcery" proclaims that He was doing actions that appeared to be miracles, and it correlates to the Pharisee's claims in the Gospel of Luke that He was doing miracles by the power of the devil (Luke 11:15). It is also stunning that it states He was "hung on the Eve of Passover" instead of stoned, which is how the gospels describe the method and time of His death. This document seems to inadvertently proclaim eyewitness testimony of Jesus' existence, trial, and means and time of death--written by the very people who were trying to defame Him.

These historical writings support Jesus' existence from around 1 BC to AD 33. A small minority of Jews trusted Him as their Messiah. They believed He was God's Son, the Messiah, incarnate in this world as Jesus of

Nazareth. The incarnate presence of Jesus changed history. His birth became the epicenter of time, and events were counted from the year He was born. He changed the world, not through war or mighty governments, like Alexander the Great or Augustus Caesar, but by dying on a cross, which was the ultimate expression of His love.

The surest and most historical way to answer questions about Jesus is by reading the writings of His disciples, who physically spent three years with Him. They wrote the only reliable, detailed, and historical accounts of Jesus' life and message, which are found in the four Gospels: Matthew, Mark, Luke, and John.

The Gospels attest to the miraculous Jesus, who was God in the flesh and who eventually sacrificed Himself and rose from the dead. The writers state that He went to the cross to take away our sins and to give us new life, providing a way to restore our relationship with God. This path of destruction was the only way for us to be reborn and reconnected to God (John 3:3–21). Jesus is portrayed as the suffering savior mentioned in Psalms 22 and Isaiah 53, the One who would heal us and free us from our transgressions.

During His short ministry, Jesus demonstrated Himself to be God through His teaching and miracles. He spent His days healing the sick, giving sight to the blind (John 1:1–38), bringing sound to the deaf (Mark 7:32–35), and raising the dead (John 11:43). It was not just a few sparse miracles; all who came to Jesus were healed (Luke 4:40). Because He was the creator of matter, He could bend it to His will. When He performed His first miracle, He changed approximately 150 gallons of washing water into fine wine (John 3:2–11). Later, He calmed a raging storm on the Sea of Galilee and invited Peter to walk on water (Mark 4:35–41, Matt. 14:24–29). He miraculously multiplied a few loaves of bread and a couple of fish to feed thousands (Matt. 14:13–21, 15:32–39). Jesus was beyond human in many demonstrable supernatural ways. His incarnation was the only time humanity ever experienced God in the flesh, whom even the wind and the waves obeyed. His greatest miracle was His own resurrection, which He regularly prophesied (John 18:22).

Jesus also embodied compassion—not only through His sacrifice on the cross but also through His daily life—resembling the healer spoken of in

Isaiah 61. The writers of the Gospels portray Jesus as loving and attentive toward the outcasts and marginalized members of society. In all His glory, He ate with sinners (Mark 2:16), touched lepers (Matt. 8:3), spoke with women (John 4:27), and spent time with children, giving them all equal importance. He demonstrated His compassion and love for the weak, the sick and the lost (Matt. 14:14).

If Jesus did so much, why was He rejected, especially since He came at a time when the Jews were expecting their Messiah? It appears that He was not what they wanted. He refused to be the kingly figure who would rise up, rid Israel of their occupying enemies, restore them to power, and establish God's kingdom on Earth. Instead of coming to overthrow Rome, Jesus came to be a suffering servant to provide a way for humanity to come to know God.

While no sign was enough for the religious rulers, the common Jews praised Jesus as Lord at His triumphal entry into Jerusalem (John 12:13).They wanted Jesus to be their Messiah and embraced Him as the king of Israel. As He rode into Jerusalem on a donkey (Zech. 9:9, John 12:15), the people shouted the messianic praise, "Blessed is he who comes in the name of the Lord" (Psalm 118:26, NKJV). They thought Jesus was the fulfillment of Zechariah's prophecy and that He would establish His earthly kingdom (Acts 1:6). Since Jesus had performed many miracles, and He had compassion for the common people in their suffering, it is no wonder that they hailed Him as their king. He valued everyone and He demonstrated a desire to have a relationship with ordinary people as He showed them the love of God. Although Jesus loved them, and they initially saw Him as the prophesied Jewish Messiah, when it became clear He would not set up His earthly kingdom, many went along with His arrest and rejection.

The leaders had understandable reasons to reject Jesus and deem Him as not qualified to be the Messiah. Born in a manger, Jesus came into the world as a lowly carpenter with no social standing, one whom the kings would conscript to die for them in a war. He was a person of insignificance as far as the rulers were concerned. How could a child of a scandalous marriage, from the mocked town of Nazareth, with no formal education and no allegiance to any party, be the ruling Messiah?

Instead of joining the ruling parties and leading a physical revolution, Jesus cleared out the temple and challenged the power of the Pharisees (Matt.

28:19), chastising them for their deception of the people (John 8:12–59). He would reconcile His people to Himself through His death on the cross and lead a spiritual revolution of love through His Spirit--not at all the physical revolt they wanted (Col. 1:20). His kingdom would be "not of this world" (John 18:36, NKJV).

Even His followers did not understand that He would not take an earthly throne and would instead die for our salvation. On their last night together, Jesus embodied the Passover supper with His closest disciples in an upper room. He taught the elements of the new covenant and spoke of His sacrificial death (John 14–16). Even after His direct teaching about His death, they still could not let go of the idea that this was the time of His rise to power. They proceeded to the Mount of Olives with Him to plot His victory, only to witness Jesus agonizing over His coming demise (Matt. 26:35-38). In the final hours of His ministry, He was betrayed and abandoned by His disciples, condemned by the Jewish rulers, rejected by the common people, and crucified by the Romans (John 18–19).

The faithful were devastated. Their belief, that Jesus was the Messiah who would establish the Jewish kingdom on Earth forever, was shattered. How could it end this way? What were they to do?

Then Jesus showed up alive again—walking, talking, and eating with His disciples. Jesus explained how He had fulfilled the Scriptures through His death and resurrection and how He provided a way to have a relationship with God for the whole world (Luke 24:27). He commissioned them to take this message everywhere and to everyone (Acts 1:8). He did not make His disciples high officials in a new earthly kingdom of power; instead, Jesus appointed them as humble workers to spread His kingdom of truth and love, reconciling people to God. They would go on to sacrifice their lives, spreading this great news: the message that God came to Earth to have a relationship with people (Matt. 28:19). Eventually, the entire world would be changed through the impact of Jesus' brief life, excruciating death on the cross, and miraculous resurrection from the dead. The message of the incarnation of God in the person of Jesus and His sacrifice to have a relationship with humanity started a fire that was—and still is—carried to the whole world by the power of the Spirit working through His followers.

This message of belief in Jesus, and transformation through the power of the Spirit, has transformed the world. The early followers in Jerusalem were deeply impacted by their experience with Jesus, which drastically changed their entire lives. They sold their excess possessions, pooled their money as a church, and shared resources according to each other's needs (Acts 2:40–47). As the salvation of individuals spread, the Spirit of Jesus began to fill the earth one heart at a time. With each newly transformed believer, evidence of love and sacrifice began to take place in the lives affected.

It was not an easy fate for this new religion and its followers. The Jewish converts were rejected by their families and communities, arrested, and sometimes murdered. Many of the non-Jewish people, who fully adopted Jesus as their God, subsequently suffered and even died for their belief in a foreign God. What kind of experience must people have had to be willing to lose all of their worldly belongings—and their lives—in defense and support of their new God? Most made these sacrifices even though they had not physically met Jesus.

Knowing the amazing effect of following Jesus, which was recorded in the Bible and in subsequent history, we are even more pressed to discover who Jesus was. Was He a scholar? A prophet? A great man? A wandering madman who claimed to be God? A revolutionary? One god of many gods? A magician or wizard? A great healer and worker of miracles (Matt. 8:16)? Merely an anomaly who said astonishing things (Matt. 5–7)? Or was Jesus who He claimed to be, the fulfillment of the prophesied Jewish Messiah? Was He God incarnate, "God with us" (Matt. 1:23, NET)? When one takes an honest look at the historical Jesus, they will find themselves tasked to make up their mind about who He was and how they will respond to His call.

Chapter 5: Is He the One?

"Are you the one who is to come, or should we look for another?"

Matthew 11:3 (NET)

THE JEWISH LEADERS at the time of Jesus were in charge of what they thought was the kingdom of God. Unwilling to surrender their structural power and convinced that He was a sorcerer doing magic by the power of Satan, they rejected Jesus of Nazareth as their Messiah because He did not fit into the religious utopia they had created.[6] They had built a life of law contrary to the grace and forgiveness Jesus offered. He did not jump through the right hoops or follow the right paths to power. Instead of joining their kingdom of God, He appeared to be against them. When the people began to follow Jesus, threatening the leader's power, they successfully sought to have Him executed.

People who lived in the Jerusalem area during the three years of Christ's ministry experienced the physical manifestation of the Son of God and were given a demonstrable choice to believe. This decision can seem more distant for us since we lack His bodily presence, yet it is ultimately the same question: will we believe in and choose to have a relationship with the man Jesus, who proved Himself to be God (John 10:24–33)? Jesus said to His disciples: "Have you believed because you have seen me? Blessed are the people who have not seen and yet have believed." (John 20:29, NET).

A belief is not just a simple decision, it is an intellectual conclusion about a reality we consider true. We surmise the best explanation of the world around us from our reason, knowledge, and observations. We choose to believe ideas and propositions that logically cohere with our experience.

Beliefs then serve as categorical assumptions about what we think is true, and they underlie our thoughts and actions. While some of these qualities may apply to how one picks their sports teams, which sports team one picks will not influence where one spends eternity or how one loves in this life.

Most of us agree on fundamental beliefs about our reality, such as the color of the sky or the smell of flowers. Beliefs like these are based predominantly on physical observations. Other beliefs are based more on inference; we may believe that our parents or spouse love us based on how they treat us. Whether sourced from observation or inference, these beliefs tend to fit into the category of things we can demonstrably reason to.

Some beliefs are more difficult for people to agree upon, such as the belief in the existence of a god or gods and convictions about their identity and character. People have difficulty agreeing on inferred beliefs because they are based less on empirically observed experiences and more on subjective observations and conclusions about the uncertain. While we may believe with extreme confidence that each time we take a step, our foot will meet solid ground, the apostle Peter would tell us that having enough belief to walk on water is a little more challenging. It is essential to consider belief in the not-so-common, maybe even allow in our thinking the possibility of occurrences beyond the natural, in order to find a deeper meaning to life.

Having a belief in the supernatural is a struggle for some because they are not willing to go beyond their own natural experience. The potential problem with using solely experience-based epistemology is that our perception and reasoning are sometimes flawed, and our experiences are limited. A lack of encounter with the supernatural does not give fact to its non-existence. If the concept of the supernatural gives you meaning and purpose, that in itself may attest to its necessity for life. While some can live without the knowledge of the supernatural and even deny it, they are left hungry for answers to questions that observation and reason cannot solve. One such question is: "Why are we reasoning creatures who value love so highly?" It is hard to believe important human attributes, like our knowledge, consciousness, and even life itself, came solely by chance, from the natural world, and not from a supernatural source.

Turning to Jesus can be much more than an intellectual decision. While Jesus was fully natural, He was also fully supernatural. We cannot get to

Jesus only by reason because He is so much more than a God we can fit within our reason. Our dilemma is that we want definitive natural proof of a mysterious supernatural reality. It is impossible to prove the supernatural through natural processes. Although, through knowing the natural, we can understand what is supernatural. Looking to science to prove God's existence or to history to prove miracles takes these disciplines beyond their scope of expertise. Yet, it is essential to know that science and history do not disprove Jesus and the miracles associated with Him.

A strong conclusion to believe and follow Jesus is rarely based on one experience or idea. Believers may have several pillars to support their belief in the supernatural truth that Jesus was the incarnate God. We may see that history presents evidence demonstrating Jesus lived a world-changing life. We may be convinced of the plausibility of the resurrection through reason. The world around us demands an intelligent and creative maker who corresponds to the description of Jesus in John's Gospel. The numerous prophecies fulfilled by Jesus point to the existence of a supernatural plan by a powerful God. Observation of Jesus' teachings proclaims wisdom beyond human ability. We may experience loneliness and emptiness that requires the Spirit as a comforter and a friend. Guilt longs for the forgiveness of the cross. Pride aches to be humbled by the true glory of God who would become a man. Pain and suffering cry out for the compassion and mercy of a savior. Evil leaves us desperate for the true love of a God who would sacrifice for us. The ramifications of believing in Jesus can bring satisfying answers to many of life's negative experiences and life's most challenging questions.

Everyone faces the same choice when encountering Jesus: will we believe Jesus was God and follow Him for our salvation? In His reflective presence, a person's true self and motives are fully displayed. It is like standing in a scanner machine at the airport. Instead of potential weapons showing up, all we have ever thought, said, or done is revealed by Jesus' presence. Having our faults revealed causes a fight-or-flight response. There is another way. We can face our brokenness. This vulnerability can only be welcomed in the presence of true love and unconditional acceptance, which is what Jesus offers us. He did not come to "condemn" us (John 3:17, NET), but to give us His love and show us "the way, and the truth, and the life" (John 14:6, NET). He wants to save us and reconcile our relationship with Him.

What is our response when we come face-to-face with the creator God—when we are forced to see our true sin-bent selves in the light of His perfect goodness and love? Jesus stands before each one of us, seeking to return us to His family as a father searches for a wayward child. We have a choice to make when we encounter the powerful, loving, and true incarnate God. Will we reject Him, or will we become His disciples and follow Him? Will we hold on to the perceived control of our less-than-adequate lives, laugh, and decide He is a madman claiming to be God, or will we take Him at His word? The tension of belief can be difficult. Can we overcome our obstacles, forsaking all we perceive as alternative answers to our deepest needs, and decide to believe in Him as the answer?

A decision to believe in and follow Jesus is how we participate in our salvation. Anyone contemplating this decision must know whether it will move them closer to comprehensively answering life's essential questions. Does it help us make sense of the world around us? Will it help us explain our own life experience in all its dimensions? Does our belief in the deity of Jesus, the truth of His teaching, and His work on the cross help us understand concepts such as love, justice, morals, relationships, joy, good, evil, consciousness, the supernatural, and existence itself? For me, a resounding "Yes" is the answer to all the above questions. The belief that Jesus is God and following Him as Savior is the greatest meaning-infusing, life-transforming decision anyone can make. Belief in Jesus' deity and His work on the cross is ultimately necessary to exist in a right and loving state with God and other humans on this earth, and it is the only promised way to be with Jesus after we die.

In order to take the final step to know the supernatural Jesus, even though we are unable to completely answer every question or intellectual objection, we often may find something other than our minds drawing us. The supernatural drawing of the Holy Spirit beckons us to respond to His simple call. He is whispering the transforming message that Jesus loves us, and He wants to make Himself known to us if only we will believe and follow Him.

I am constrained by Jesus to directly ask you, the reader, this question: Confronted with the existence of Jesus, will you accept that He was the supernatural answer to your existential questions, or will you brush Him off as a natural phenomenon puffed up by His disciples? One may attempt to delay their response until they are certain of the facts by searching the world's religions, studying what the great philosophers have said, or researching history and science to find assurance to His reality and His claims. I completely relate to this because searching for certainty is not a weakness but a necessity, yet it is a never-ending, unfulfilling quest. It always brought me back to the same question that we all face. Everyone must decide what they believe about Jesus because the incarnation and the cross cannot be ignored. After your search, you are still left to decide for yourself what is accurate regarding His being God and whether He resurrected from the dead. In the end, it may not be your intellect that brings you to a final decision to follow Jesus; instead, it may be an insatiable need for a creator who loves you, forgives you, and wants desperately to have a relationship with you.

If you feel drawn to Him, for whatever reason, you do not need to solve every objection. No one can know all knowledge and what the future will bring, so you are left to embrace your current experience and understanding, trusting the future will bring similar problems and answers. This is how people move forward on a variety of essential decisions where there is no possibility of complete certainty, and it is how you can take the supernatural step toward Jesus, away from a life without Him––even if you cannot know everything definitively.

If and when we decide to believe, we can be assured of our supernatural transition by what Paul wrote to the first-century church in Rome: "If you declare with your mouth, 'Jesus is Lord,' and believe in your heart that God raised him from the dead, you will be saved" (Rom. 10:9, NIV). Declaring Jesus is Lord and believing in our hearts that God raised Him from the dead becomes a monumental belief that can bring a life-changing transformation.

The faith you exercise when you believe in Jesus is not irrational. Belief in the supernatural Jesus for salvation is far from irrational because His followers find it a necessity of life. Once someone decides to follow Jesus and experiences the way of love, knowledge of the truth, and new life in His Spirit, it becomes the only rational conclusion imaginable.

You can make the decision to believe in Jesus as complicated as you like, but the complication is unnecessary. It can be a simple decision to believe in the Lord Jesus because you recognize that He is the way to fill the void inside, to explain and heal your pain, and the way to answer life's biggest questions—questions you have been asking all your life. When you believe in the Lord Jesus, you are given a new, abundant life with Him here and now, and a future eternal life in His presence.

Chapter 6: Jesus is the Source of a Good Life

And this is the testimony: God has given us eternal life, and this life is in his Son. Whoever has the Son has life; whoever does not have the Son of God does not have life.

First John 5:11–12 (NIV)

I FIRST ASKED JESUS to save me the summer before my fifth birthday. At such a young age, how did I get to the place where I needed to be saved? The book of Genesis teaches God created us like Himself, making creatures with whom He desired to share eternity (Gen. 3:22–24). Adam and Eve ate the fruit of rebellion and chose to go it alone without God. When they transgressed, they started the moral fall that facilitated a separation from the God of love, our intimate teacher and Father. Even at almost five, I sensed I needed to be saved from who I had become and the bad things I did. I wanted to know my creator who lo, and I needed to stop building my kingdom with no place for God in it. Most of all, just like everyone else, I needed His life restored in me if I was going to live a *good life*.

When I accepted Christ, I wanted someone to love me as Jesus did—I also did not want to go to Hell. A child may not understand fully, but as we grow, it is vital to understand the truths of our salvation. It is not merely adding Jesus to our life for self-benefit and receiving fire insurance for the next. Choosing to follow Jesus involves immediately restoring a relationship with the Father and then beginning a journey towards restoring His love and knowledge as our guide to life. Our transformation starts by confronting our self-centeredness, which leads to hate and evil, and then placing Jesus as our cornerstone, which leads to self-sacrificing love. When we choose Jesus, we are embracing His kingdom, abandoning a life lived by our knowledge of good and evil, and living the eternal life that the Spirit brings with Jesus at the center.

If the above is true, then salvation in Jesus is not a process of relying on systems such as organized religion, family structures, government solutions, or self-help strategies to transform our lives. Many of these systems are somewhat beneficial but also can be a form of slavery to burdensome tasks that attempt to fix our old, dead selves. Although well-intentioned, they cannot bring freedom from the brokenness that stems from sin and separation from God.

The freedom salvation brings comes from God restoring life in us—the life and relationship lost when Adam went his own way (1 Cor. 15:22). God does this by removing sin from us and restoring the presence of His (Gal. 3:14). is Jesus in us and ourselves in Him that restores life. John wrote: "And this is the testimony: God has given us eternal life, and this life is in his Son. Whoever has the Son has life; whoever does not have the Son of God does not have life" (1 John 5:11–12, NIV). We cannot have this new life, the means of salvation, if we do not have the source of the new life in us, which is the indwelling of the Son of God.

Having the source of the *good life* in us is predicated on Him declaring us righteous by forgiving and removing our sins through His death on the cross. We may ask: have we all committed sins so terrible we deserve to be tortured and crucified? We may not think so, but the destructive results of our sins, even though they may not warrant such severe punishment, cannot be overlooked. Jesus' gruesome death was capable of overcoming the life-destroying results of our sins, no matter how destructive they were and are. We are all in need of the salvation provided on the cross. Our forgiveness is realized, and we are declared righteous when we accept His suffering and death on the cross as a substitute for the penalty of death we deserve (1 John 1:9, 4:10; Acts 10:43; Col. 2:13–15).

The cross was the means of restoring His life in us. It was where love and mercy appeased justice to provide forgiveness of sins to all who believe. His willingness to die also demonstrated the incredible forgiveness and sacrificial love we are to embody toward others and ourselves. Jesus went to the cross not only to give us love, mercy, and forgiveness but also to bring healing and restoration. He wanted to restore our relationship with our creator and with one another. Living the way of the cross, with the Spirit living in us, will transform our lives and begin our journey to live a *good life* (Col. 1:27).

What does this salvific transformation look like? When Paul told the Philippian jailor that he and his household would be saved, did he mean they would know Jesus, or did he mean the Romans would not kill them for failing at his post? What does salvation mean for us today? Let's look at some common questions about its effect on our lives.

Will salvation make us into a person people like? As we become more loving, we will gain friends—some will be sincere, and some will be takers. We all find it difficult when believers don't live by Jesus' love. Without seeking His Spirit to change us with His truth and love, one may not grow or might even get worse. It gets very complicated to quantify if a person is changing if they are not living by the Spirit.

Well, doesn't God, at the very least, make us happy? Yes, He can make a person happy, but happiness is only one of the myriads of human emotions. A *good life* consists of much more than happiness. Life is composed of experiencing what the ABC television company used to proclaim about sports, "The thrills of victory and the agony of defeat." In many endeavors, there is only one winner—only one person or team among the many gets the trophy. The truth of salvation changes our understanding of what a winner is and realigns our priorities on the road to true joy.

Many things bring a new source of happiness to our lives. A fundamental element is having community and friends in the church. We are given a new perspective on others, learning that beauty is only skin deep and that a person's love for others and their love for God is what matters most. These truths and others will free us from the world's deceptions about happiness. Still, depression, anxiety, and other mental illnesses are real and often untreatable diseases of the flesh. People with brain ailments must work harder to find this new joy God promises. God's will is for all to have His joy, but it appears slow to come for some.

The church is an integral part of this new life. It is a type of family where brothers and sisters love on one another. The truth and love found in the body of Christ on earth can be life changing. Although the church is a tool God uses, one must not forget that it is full of broken people who make hurtful mistakes. The *good life* Jesus brings into our lives is enhanced by the church as much as the church demonstrates His love. We need to find a church that is teaching the truth of our salvation and living the love of Jesus.

Does God save us from our diseases? The obvious answer for me and many others is a resounding no. Even after much prayer, I continue to suffer from psoriasis and psoriatic arthritis. My father had severe arthritis for half of his adult life. My mother had dementia, suffered from mini-strokes, and died from complications of a major stroke. We all die. Yes, there are times when God heals us temporarily to make us more comfortable and prolong our lives, but eventually, we must go home. It's important to understand that the Father's will is not for us to suffer, yet "In this world we will have trouble" (John 16:33, NIV). Jesus overcame the world by demonstrating that submitting to a His loving Father's will is the way to transcend our troubles. He also gives us the Spirit to help us endure and grow from our hardships. Jesus provided us a way through our struggle, not a way out of it. A *good life* is a life lived in the light of His truth, with His love demonstrated in all the circumstances we find ourselves in.

Will more money make our lives better? To help answer the question about how much money we should have, it's essential to know God is not a piggy bank. Many Christians are poor, which does not mean they don't have faith, or that God doesn't love them. Jesus said, "Blessed are you who are poor..." (Luke 6:20, NET). The poor are blessed with the gift of dependence on God; they seek God for every meal and don't have a nest egg they trust in. They don't walk around thinking they have it all together and that God is blessing them since they are so successful. They also tend to be generous givers because they know what it is like to need. As you can see, having money your whole life can rob you of many experiences. In Fidler on the Roof, when Perchik states that "money is the world's curse!" Tevye responds: "May the Lord smite me with it, and may I never recover!" How much is enough money for God to smite us with? Our appetite seems rarely satisfied; if it ever is—we will wake up the next day and want more tomorrow.

I know of no examples of salvation increasing someone's intelligence, but in almost every instance, the truth of salvation makes people wiser. Even more importantly, it tends to make people kinder. Of course, kindness is on a scale, but after being forgiven, we hope that people would intern be kinder to the less fortunate. There are so many little things like wisdom and kindness that the Spirit manifests in our lives. The small things make a big difference as we walk in His love.

One thing salvation does for everyone is provide a way of contentment, which should rid us of greed and coveting. I say "should" because very few of us can walk without regard for the world's treasures. It is made more difficult when we are hungry, thirsty, unsuccessful, or our health fails. With the world, nothing is ever enough. With Christ, He alone is enough.

Something salvation does not appear to do is make Christians moral according to the Law of Moses or any other laws. There are plenty of Christians in prison from breaking the law and a plethora of pastors and priests who have abused their flock. I scream out in this book that living by the Spirit, who teaches us to love as Jesus loves, will make us moral, loving people, but that is a life process that many Christians never start. Believers tend to be enslaved to the religion of Christianity, which promotes following the law to be righteous. The way of Jesus is a perfect moral system, but people will never be able to follow it perfectly. Some, even with Jesus, stray away and behave more like the Devil.

Does God forgive all our sins? Yes! Despite its importance, forgiveness of our sins is not the whole of our salvific transformation. At the cross, Jesus also removed the law that defined our sins to condemn us. When we follow Jesus, we are set free from bondage to the law of sin and death, and instead, we live by the law of the Spirit (Rom. 8:1-2). We begin the path to a new and *good life* when we live by the law of truth and love written on our hearts by His presence in us.

Salvation does set us free: "It is for freedom that Christ has set us free" (Gal. 5:1, NIV). On the surface, this does not seem apparent. There have been enslaved Christians throughout the centuries, and even free people don't escape oppression by someone or something in their lives, whether it be a parent, boss, spouse, government, or even one's life circumstances. Freedom in the flesh is on a continuum. In Christ, we are free no matter what our outside circumstances may be. We are free from living by the written law when we choose to live by the law of the Spirit. The law condemns and brings death, but the law of the Spirit brings life and love. Our freedom is first and foremost realized in our spirit, and from that, our freedom flows out of us into the world around us. So many martyrs faced death, tied to a stake, ready to be burned, yet they were free because they lived out His truth and His love. Their true freedom could not be taken from them.

God is the author of our salvation, and we are to discover it "with fear and trembling." (Phil. 2:12, NKJV). It's not easy to walk in His mysterious plan for our lives with all of the world's distractions in our immediate focus. We somewhat walk in blindness, yet we are not blind to the knowledge that the Spirit's main concern is that we manifest His gift of love (1 John 4:7; Rom. 5:5). God transforms our lives as we work out our new path, bringing a new destiny and purpose. We are freed from looking to the world, others, and ourselves for the way to live and godly life and are given the Spirit who guides us in the truth and love as we walk in our new relationship with Him.

Even with everything that salvation through Christ's death provides, we may still suffer in the flesh due to the chaos of this world, our mistakes, humanity's failures, and other people's destructive behaviors (Rom. 1:18–32). We must also remember that "our struggle is not against flesh and blood, but against the powers and principalities" in the spiritual realm. We know little about this realm, but that it is there, and that it negatively affects us. Satan wants to control us so that His will is ruling the world and not the Father's.

While we will never escape our troubles in the physical realm, belief in Jesus can free us and relieve us of our internal condemnation from sin if we let it. Even more, as we live by the Spirit, He transforms our outward interactions to reflect what Jesus has done for us on the inside. Jesus does save us in so many ways, yet maybe not always how we expect Him to. In the Lord's Prayer, we pray for the Father's will to be done, not ours.

Despite the battles that life, Satan, and the world rage against us, salvation in Jesus changes our lives. It perfectly relates to the human spirit, healing and forgiving us. It brings freedom from sin, guilt, shame, and punishment, and it brings freedom to be who God wants us to be, without the shackles of the past or a fear of the future. Even more so, His salvation imparts us with new life as He manifests His love through the indwelling of the Spirit. The Spirit makes His home in us (John 14:20), and we start to become a beautiful work of art. God takes our broken and tattered lives (Rom. 7:24; Eph. 2:1–7) and begins to perfect them in His love (1 John

2:5, 4:12, 17–18; 2 Cor. 5:17). As we walk with Jesus and listen to the Spirit, we embark on a new life! We are living on an entirely new path of grace, love, and the knowledge of the truth—away from our previous path of destruction. When we believe in the Good News of Jesus, we are saved from our destiny of destruction. Our lives are transformed both in this life and in the next, and we are given the source for having a *good life* when we live our lives love side up. The end of Part 1.

To further your quest for the *good life,* read your Bible, pray, and find a loving church that teaches from the Bible about grace, truth, and the love of Jesus. You can also read parts 2 and 3 of the full book, Love Side Up: The Secret to Living a Good Life if you would like to continue to read my insights on the matter.

APPENDIX to Part 1: The Fate of Those Who Don't Follow Jesus

In the same way, your Father in heaven is not willing that one of these little ones be lost.

Matthew 18:14 (NET)

And he himself is the atoning sacrifice for our sins, and not only for our sins but also for the whole world.

First John 2:2 (NET)

CHRISTIANS ARE CALLED to love as Jesus loved, which means to love and have compassion for all, with a desire for every person to have a relationship with Jesus. This compulsion to love others and lead them to Jesus seems to conflict with the apparent Scripture teaching that everyone without Jesus is going to an eternal place of suffering. That is a sad, horrific thought that, at face value, does not appear loving, just, or compassionate. Unfortunately, without the eternal life that comes from believing in Jesus, humans will not go to be with Him when they die and instead will go to reside in hell until the final judgment. In hell, they will face judgment and punishment for their destructive choices in their life. The question I am contemplating in this chapter is: After suffering in hell, could God show His mercy, love, and compassion towards some non-believers?

Most religions attempt to teach the way to peace in the afterlife. Many of them practice some version of merit-based righteousness and conditional grace. Merit-based righteousness is performing redemptive obligations to be right with God. Works of service, doing good deeds, and repenting of one's failures become ways to receive forgiveness and mercy in this life and the transition to the next. This is the path of conditional grace. Adherents to religions hope fairness and mercy will be given when they are judged but have little certainty about whether they have done enough to warrant this grace.

The Hebrews, who used the Mosaic law given by God, were the closest to having the perfect system of merit-based righteousness, with the hope of receiving God's grace in the afterlife for their faith and obedience. Other Abrahamic-sourced religions, including the Latter-day Saints (the Mormons) and the Muslims, have interesting and somewhat successful plans as well. Eastern religions, such as Hinduism, Buddhism, and Confucianism, also have attractive teachings on how to find balance in this life and the possibility of improving their lot in the next. Even some variations of Christianity preach and practice a form of conditional grace when they teach obligations to keep one's salvation in the right standing.

In light of this dilemma, religious pluralists have made a noble attempt to answer the question: What is the eternal fate of good and loving people who may have contradictory paths to God? Pluralists tend to blend religions by synchronizing overlapping ideas and downplaying the differences. They contend most religions describe a way to encounter the same deity. Their blending leads to embracing universal salvation for all who follow a god and are decently behaved, or they sometimes promote the idea of salvation for everyone, depending on the sect.

Pluralism even exists in Christianity. When one accepts Jesus as their primary way to heaven but also is open to other possibilities of salvation, they are a Christian pluralist. This sentiment serves to ease the Christian's worry about the non-believer's fate in the afterlife by including the possibility that more people will go to heaven than just a small number of Jesus' followers. In the movie *Life of Pi*, although Pi professed Christianity, he also believed all religions combined into a beautiful symphony, and this idea was presented in a convincing and appealing way. Universal salvific ideas may seem loving and attractive, yet they contradict what the Bible says about the way to God, in addition to downplaying what the other religions say concerning salvation.

Whether a person is a Mormon, a Muslim, a Hindu, a Jew, a religious Christian who practices works salvation, or they find some other method of achieving promised bliss in the afterlife, they are following a religious system of good and evil and their perceived potential in the next life is based on their merit. The actual ability to enter the presence of God and inherit eternal life comes solely based on the righteousness Jesus gives us, which makes us worthy to be with Him. Christ did not come to harmonize with the religions of the world; He came to end religions and their laws and replace them with simply believing in and following Jesus with His Spirit in us. Despite religion's beauty, wisdom, and power to restrain sin and encourage us to love our neighbor, it is not the way of eternal life described in the New Testament.

The Bible clearly states no one comes to the Father except through the Son, Jesus (John 14:6). This means Jesus' death—the shedding of His blood to cover our sins—is the only means by which anyone can enter the presence of God. If the Father does not apply the blood of Jesus to cover our sins, we are not made righteous, and we are not worthy to go to heaven, where God resides. Scripture makes no exceptions for anyone's entrance to heaven, at death, without Christ's blood, except maybe the children of Christian parents. In Paul's first letter to the Corinthians, he alludes to the idea that they will go to heaven (1 Cor. 7:14). But, in understanding righteousness, we know it would still require the Father to apply Christ's blood to them. It is also reasonable to believe the Father applied the blood of Jesus to the saints who lived prior to the cross—otherwise, no one who lived before Christ would be able to be in the presence of God. Whether religious or non-religious, anyone without Jesus exists under the old covenant of merit-based righteousness and conditional mercy. Anyone who did not or does not know Jesus cannot know whether the Father will extend His mercy to them by applying Jesus' death to take away their sins and allow them to avoid the lake of fire (1 John 5:11-12). The Bible states that they will go to hell when they die, but their fate at the final judgment is uncertain.

Understanding the gravity of eternal separation from God, knowing the relatively small group of people who follow Jesus, and considering the apparent unfairness for those who have not had a clear opportunity to accept Christ, a typical Evangelical Christian may want to make exceptions to the rule that following Jesus is the only way to avoid hell and eternal punishment.

One such exception commonly made is regarding children. This exception is implemented by establishing an age of accountability, which can biblically be as high as twenty (Num. 14:29). If a child dies under the age of accountability, it is suggested the child will go to heaven to be with Jesus, even if they have not chosen to follow Him. Other exceptions might be made for loving people who have not heard the gospel and for those who are too mentally incapacitated to comprehend or to make such a choice. Few would accept the condemnation of the souls lost to abortion, even though they did not choose to follow Jesus. There are sometimes exceptions made for moral, loving people, not of the Christian religion, who devoutly believe in God but who have had no chance to turn to Jesus. Even among the thousands of different sects of Christianity, believers carve out exceptions for all the varying methods of salvation in Jesus, not wanting to be dogmatic about their way being precisely correct. How much will God hold people, even Christians, accountable for this confusion? Who will be spared from hell and the lake of fire at the final judgment?

If Christians are going to speculate about God's mercy toward some who did not choose—or did not have the chance—to follow Jesus, we should be scripturally and logically consistent. I do not promote Christian pluralism or any universal way of salvation when I contemplate the idea of God giving grace in the end to some individuals who did not accept Jesus. What I am suggesting is that while there is no option to avoid hell, there may be some way to avoid eternal punishment. While all people are only saved by the blood of Christ, the Father can apply the Son's gift of grace to whomever He decides, even if they did not choose to believe in and follow Christ in this life. Whether we think He gives grace to pre-Christ saints, to babies, to children, to "good" people who have not heard, or to anyone else, we should be able to consistently articulate our views on God's mercy concerning the salvation of unbelievers.

The idea of God giving grace to those who did not accept Jesus is a big hurdle for many Christians. Most would argue that, beyond young children and the incapacitated, few are truly worthy of being saved based on their merit, especially if they reject Jesus. In Romans 3:23 (NIV), Paul writes, "For all have sinned and fall short of the glory of God." He wrote earlier in verse 3:10 (NIV), "There is no one righteous, not even one." Sin separates us from

God, and we can do nothing to change that. All our religious efforts are futile attempts at obtaining God's favor. Paul wrote that even Abraham was saved by his faith, not his works (Rom. 4:3). Merit means nothing regarding going to heaven to be with Jesus when one dies.

Again, I agree that those without Jesus will go to hell. What is different in what I am saying is that God may have a way of giving grace and mercy at the final judgment. This does not in any way support the idea that people can go to heaven to be with Jesus when they die if they are good enough in life.

When we conclude that all unbelievers will go to hell when they die, we are still faced with an important question: Will all in hell suffer their entire time there, or is there also still a place of rest? God is a gracious and just judge, and I cannot honestly say how He will punish those who have not had a chance to receive His Son or decided not to believe. I can only guess that they will be judged justly according to their works and their belief in a God they may not have fully known. God says:

> I, the Lord, probe into people's minds. I examine people's hearts. I deal with each person according to how he has behaved. I give them what they deserve based on what they have done.
>
> Jeremiah 17:10 (NET)

According to this verse, when people die, they will be judged and given the punishment they deserve. Whatever the punishment is, justice will demand that it is different in severity and length for everyone. For some, as in the case of babies and young children, if they reside in hell, I assert there will be no suffering, only rest until the final resurrection and judgment.

For God to be just and loving and to keep heaven pure, an existence away from heaven that contains a place of punishment, and a place of rest seems a necessary state for all who are not pure or who have not been made righteous. For those who have done little or no wrong, even though they do not have Jesus, it makes sense that they would be sent to a place of rest other than heaven. As Jeremiah indicates in the verse quoted above, those who have done evil will suffer their just punishment. It is highly possible that after people pay for their wrongs, they may spend the remainder of their time before the final judgment in the place of rest.

You may wonder why I insist that those without Jesus are going to reside in hell and will encounter rest or suffering. If a person is a sinner and does not have Jesus, there is no place in heaven for them. No one is worthy of being in God's presence if they have not put their faith in Jesus to take away their sins. By presenting hell as a place of punishment and rest, I am attempting to harmonize what is said about hell and salvation in all of Scripture. Hell could be a horrifying place for some and peaceful for others (Luke 16:22-27). Justice would demand that it is a place where we get what we deserve: "And as it is appointed unto men once to die, but after this judgment" (Heb. 9:27, KJV). Justice will be sentenced in the afterlife if not fully served in this life for all who do evil and to those who choose to reject God's gift of eternal life in Christ Jesus. The Bible teaches that those without Christ are not going to heaven, yet it does not condemn all in hell to a place of torture but perhaps to a place of appropriate punishment or appropriate rest (Luke 23:43; Heb. 9:27).

Therefore, although people without Jesus go to reside in hell, they are not all in a bad place; some are in a comfortable place of waiting. We know of the place of rest from Jesus' teaching. He taught that hell is made up of a place of suffering and a place that He referred to as Paradise. This is especially made clear by His response to the thief on a cross (Luke 16:22-26, 23:43). As he was dying, Jesus said to the thief, "today you will be with me in paradise" (Luke 23:43, NET).Jesus Himself descended into hell and did not go to a place of punishment but to rest (Matt. 12:40). Paradise at that time was the place of rest in hell where people were spared from punishment, also called "Abraham's Bosom" in the parable of Lazarus and the rich man (Luke 16:23).

The idea of moral, loving people going to a place of rest if they do not have eternal life is more consistent in communicating God's justice and grace than Christians merely picking and choosing which people, who do not believe in Jesus, the Father will take to heaven (with no scriptural basis for their assumptions). Jesus' response to the thief on a cross next to Him, when He gave the guilty thief mercy at the very last hour of his life, illustrates God's compassionate heart in sending some to paradise (Luke 23:39-43). Jesus did this while He was suffering greatly as an innocent man. Can you imagine how hard it would be to love in those circumstances? If God's judgment is anything like the compassion shown to the thief, who are we to preclude His compassion to give others a chance to be in paradise?

We have examples of God's mercy to explain the salvation of people prior to knowledge and acceptance of the gospel. All the saints of the Old Testament are believed to be saved, such as Adam, Seth, Enoch, Methuselah, Noah, Job, Terah, Abraham, Isaac, Jacob, Moses, and all those who lived by faith in Yahweh (Heb. 11:1-12:1). Ninevites and others mentioned in the Bible repented and followed the true God. Were they only saved in this life temporarily and then sent eternally to suffer, or were they given mercy in the afterlife as well? What happens to all the tribes and cultures who appear to have lost all knowledge of the true God? Is a belief in the Great Spirit enough, such as some of the Native American tribes believe? Before cultures had the written word, the process of correct universal beliefs must have been much different and subject to greater error. A just and merciful God would have a plan to accommodate this reality. A place of suffering, along with a place of rest, would do just that.

So then, what is the final fate for those in the place of rest? Although those in paradise do not immediately receive eternal life and go to be with Jesus, a future opportunity to choose to follow Jesus would not be out of the question in terms of fairness and mercy. Any chance for a pardon for the condemned would entirely depend on God extending His grace by covering their sins with Christ's blood. The possibility of grace after death was traditionally called postmortem evangelism and was believed by some early church fathers until Augustine.[7] While this particular argument for a second chance is not exactly what they believed, it is along some of the same lines of thinking—attempting to understand God's mercy and grace for those who did not have a chance to believe. The possibility of future mercy for those in paradise is more consistent with a just, fair, and loving God. It makes the doctrine of salvation through Jesus alone more understandable, considering the reality of the large number of people who die without the opportunity to know Jesus.

Practically, this works out as follows. For non-believers, there are two judgments in the Scriptures: once when they die (Heb. 9:27), and then the final judgment at the great white throne (Rev. 20:11-15; John 5:28-30; Acts 24:14-15). When believers die, we are not judged (1 John 5:11-12; John 3:36; 5:24), although we will be purified (1 Cor. 3:12-15), and we go to be with Jesus until the second resurrection (1 Thess. 4:14). All who die after the cross, without Jesus, will be judged and reside in hell for a minimum of one thousand years during the millennium. So, if you were to die today without Christ, you would be in hell until the return of Jesus and the resurrection of believers, plus an additional one thousand years during the reign of Christ. Most will not suffer during this entire time but will live out their deserved punishment and then be remediated to a place of rest. This limited suffering is what I believe God's justice—combined with God's love, mercy, and compassion—would dictate. The opportunity for postmortem grace would transpire at the end of this time.

The second chance for those in paradise most likely occurs at the final rebellion, after which their fate will be made known at the great white throne judgment (Rev. 20:12). To understand the second chance fully, we need to look at the end of Christ's reign—John prophecies in the Book of Revelation about a rebellion after a thousand years (Rev. 20:7-15).

> When the thousand years are completed, Satan will be released from his prison, and will come out to deceive the nations which are in the four corners of the earth, Gog and Magog, to gather them together for the war; the number of them is like the sand of the seashore.
>
> Revelation 20:7-8 (NASB)

Rebellion implies that people will be given the ability to choose for or against Jesus, who will be king at that time. For years, I wondered why anybody would choose against Jesus. One of the primary purposes of the rebellion is to give the people in paradise one last chance to decide whether to follow Jesus or rebel. Not all will follow Jesus, for it says in the rebellion Satan will bring a "number of them ...like the sand of the seashore." It is very likely that this "number" comes from the living and the dead.

Those who do not choose Jesus, along with Satan, will be defeated, judged, and cast into the lake of fire; whether that is annihilation or eternal suffering, we do not know. Jesus Himself spoke of the final judgment when He spoke of the dead being resurrected and judged based on their works:

> A time is coming when all who are in their graves will hear His voice and come out—those who have done what is good will rise to live, and those who have done what is evil will rise to be condemned.
>
> John 5:28-29 (NIV)

The parable of the sheep and the goats is another picture of the final judgment (Matt. 25:31-46). In it, Jesus proclaims that people with the right heart and motives will be pardoned. This is a parable about the judgment of non-Christians and not about judgment for those who follow Jesus. He said we will not be judged as believers but instead pass immediately from death to life (John 5:24). It would be hard to reconcile the sheep and goats as representing Christians and deceived Christians. If it were about Christians, who can know if anyone is saved? Instead, those without Jesus appear to be judged based on their acts of love and service, and their religion is not even mentioned. This parable clearly says some who did not accept Jesus in their first life are given a second chance based on their loving actions after they have suffered for their sins. Whether based on good works or choosing Christ at the final rebellion, some are spared from the lake of fire, and their names are found in the "Book of Life" (Rev. 20:15, NKJV).

John prophesied in the book of Revelation concerning the final judgment:

> And I saw the dead, small and great, standing before God, and books were opened. And another book was opened, which is the Book of Life. And the dead were judged according to their works, by the things which were written in the books. ...Then Death and Hades were cast into the lake of fire. This is the second death. And

anyone not found written in the Book of Life was cast into the lake of fire.

Revelation 20:12,14-15 (NKJV)

This is the final judgment when the realms of Earth and hell will be purged of evil and evildoers. Notice that the "dead" are judged. This cannot refer to believers, for we are alive in Christ Jesus.

I trust in God's final judgment. He is a merciful, loving, and just God who will judge fairly. If we humans think we can be fair judges of good and evil, how can we question God's final decisions regarding who will be in the Book of Life? Of the two ways to get in, one is simple, and the other is extremely long, hard, and not guaranteed. One is granted and sealed by accepting Christ and happens immediately upon our belief; the other is based on mere speculation about God's judgment and relying on His fairness, justice, and mercy. For the non-Christian, the final decision about one's fate is only revealed at the final judgment, after the thousand-year reign of Christ and the great rebellion.

Knowing the possibility of a second chance at redemption helps us explain to people the life they can have in Jesus Christ in comparison to the punishment they will have without Him and the uncertainty of their final destination. It is also comforting to know there is some hope for all the guilty people who die without Jesus. Although they will justly receive punishment for the wrongs they have committed, they will eventually be remitted to paradise and be given a second chance to be redeemed. In contrast, innocent people who die without Jesus will immediately receive rest in paradise and find salvation when the Book of Life is opened. There is little reason to cast a certain horrific picture of the afterlife for those who do not have a chance to accept Jesus. Scripture is clear: everyone who does not believe in Jesus will go to hell and be judged, but that judgment will be justly and fairly carried out by a benevolent God. In the very end, when the Book of Life is opened, only the Father knows the names of the unredeemed that will be spared from the lake of fire.

PART 2: THE JOURNEY TO A GOOD LIFE

Foreword to Part 2

I have come so that you may have life, and may have it abundantly.

John 10:10 (NET)

OUR UNDERSTANDING OF the truth and impact of salvation cannot be exhausted, yet it is not an endless quest. At a foundational level, the gospel is so simple a child can understand it. For some, this new life is the precious gift of walking with Jesus daily in His love, and that is enough. Others are moved by the Spirit to unravel the mysteries of the gospel and its implications for their lives. For most of us, the journey lies somewhere between. Understanding the simplicity of salvation is extremely important, but knowing more about the grace and truth Jesus imparts to us is also helpful to continue to grow, empowering us to experience the promised *good life* (John 10:10).

The journey to experience a *good life* begins with understanding the work Jesus did on the cross. He brought a paradigm shift to how one lives their life when He modeled sacrificial love by willingly dying for our salvation. He possessed more power and wisdom than anyone who had ever lived, yet He did not use it to rule the world. Instead, He suffered to create a relationship with humanity. Understanding this reason-defying act from a new perspective enhances our sense of how Jesus changes our lives and defines our purpose as His followers in a confusing world. What Christ accomplished on the cross frees us to live by the Spirit and opens a whole new life for us.

The apostle Paul wrote that this new life of freedom is not the old life of living by the "law of sin and death"—it is a new life lived by the "law of the Spirit of life" (Rom. 8:2, NKJV). The apostle John explained how to live by the "law of the Spirit of life" when he wrote: "If we love one another, God abides in us, and His love is perfected in us" (1 John 4:12, NKJV).

If we want to experience this transforming power of the cross, we need to understand sanctification in our lives through the love of the cross. This means emulating Jesus' love as you live by the power of the Spirit in you. He is the one who teaches us the truth of the gospel and instructs us daily on how to love.

Our transformation begins with following Jesus as Lord. Still, the richness of understanding our new ability to emulate the love Jesus showed on the cross—through the power of the Spirit—is the essence of how the *good life* is lived out. Living in the love of the cross is an upside-down way to live according to a world that champions strength and possessions. Jesus came to turn the world *love-side-up* by forever changing the lives of those who embrace the *good life* lived with the love of the cross.

Chapter 7: Using the Right Fuel

For the law of the life-giving Spirit in Christ Jesus has set you free from the law of sin and death.

Romans 8:2 (NET)

TRAVELING IN A CAR makes for a fitting illustration of living the Christian life by the Spirit. Consider how difficult it would be to push a car down the road instead of using fuel. Trying to live the Christian life through religious actions without the power of the Spirit is similarly unwise. While Christian institutions can aid our attempts to love better by instructing us in what is good, evil, foolish, and wise, the moral imperatives promoted are not the fuel source for our new life; they are not what makes us intentionally good. Just like it doesn't matter how long you stare at the speedometer in your car or how well you know the speed limit, it will not make you go faster or slower. Adjusting the fuel source through the pedal is what changes the car's speed. Our fuel for sanctification, our movement towards having Jesus' love dominate our hearts and actions, is the Holy Spirit, not the dashboard of potential rules we find in various sects of Christianity. Surprising to most, it is not even the descriptions of behaviors to pursue or avoid found in the Bible. Only through following the Spirit can we accomplish the movement promised and find ourselves going in the right direction. Moving steadily along life's highway, with the Spirit as our fuel, is the right way to live life as a Christian.

The Spirit keeps us in the middle of the road by teaching us His truth and moving us to love without judging by the law. On one side of the road is rebellion and hate, where one indulges in evil, selfish, and hurtful acts. If we drive off this side of the road, we agree that the law is an effective tool to inform us of our distance from truth and love. Only God's Spirit and love can bring us back to the center of the road without throwing us off to the other side. The other side of the road is religion, where one lives by religious rules to become sanctified. This diversion contains law, judgment, guilt, shame, and punishment. It represents slavery to the law of sin and death, in which good works become our righteousness, and our failures estrange us from God's love. Again, only God's Spirit and love can bring us back to the middle of the road without sending us off to the other side of rebellion.

The Spirit empowers us to live Jesus' example of love and keeps our lives centered on the truth. If we look to sin or religion, just as when driving a car, we will go in the direction we look and fail to live by the Spirit in the center. In his letter to the Romans, Paul wrote about being a slave to sin in chapter six, living by the law in chapter seven, and living by the Spirit in chapter eight. God wants us right in the middle of the highway, living by His Spirit, learning the knowledge of our salvation, and practicing the love of Jesus.

Freedom from living according to Mosaic law and New Testament rules is difficult for most to understand. Asserting we live by the Spirit, who teaches and guides us to enact His love instead of following rules, makes some believers uncomfortable. Jesus taking away our sins (Rom. 6:6, 8:1–2, 11:27; Heb. 10:17–18; 1 John 3:5; John 1:29), not just the punishment, requires the removal of the written law. Fear of taking away the law and other lists of sin should be alleviated by the knowledge we are indwelt by the Holy Spirit, who is perfecting us in His love.

The prophet Jeremiah described the Spirit in us, functioning as our new guide to sanctification through truth and love:

> "Behold, days are coming," declares the Lord, "when I will make a new covenant ...I will put My law within them and on their heart I will write it; and I will be their God, and they shall be My people. They will not teach again, each man his neighbor and each man his brother, saying, 'Know the Lord,' for they will all know Me, from the least of them to the greatest of them," declares the Lord, "for I will forgive their iniquity, and their sin I will remember no more."

Jeremiah 31:31, 33–34 (NASB)

Jeremiah states the law will be written on the hearts of God's people, and their sins will be remembered no more. This prophecy is applied explicitly to Christians by the writer of Hebrews. He quotes this passage from the book of Jeremiah, emphasizing that the Spirit leads each one of us in the way that is right. This goes against the idea and practice that Christians need to be taught every Sunday to fix their sins. If we have the Spirit in our hearts as our guide, why do we depend so heavily on rules and standards to point out our sins and control our behavior?

You've likely heard the expression, "Rome wasn't built in a day." The Jews protested with a similar sentiment about the temple taking forty-six years to build when Jesus claimed He could rebuild it in three days. This claim framed an interesting comparison of religion's work in our lives versus the work of the Spirit. The Jewish temple, the place where God communed with man, took years to build. Jesus made this relationship possible for all mankind in only three days—actually, in one night.

In my walk with God, it took me forty-six years to begin to practice the reality that my new goodness and righteousness come solely from Him. Sadly, I was building my own religious kingdom, which got in the way of the Spirit's work in my life. Living by His Spirit, not by using a list of rules to judge or punish others and myself, freed me from my anger and from an instinct to condemn. Living a Spirit-filled life means living with the continual awareness of God's love for us, His forgiveness given to us, and His freedom to love Him back, love ourselves well, and sacrificially love others. This way of living with the Spirit brings the kingdom of God to Earth—a kingdom of truth and love in our hearts, minds, and lives—it is not a utopian kingdom of rules and good deeds that humans may conceive.

Changing one's beliefs and perspectives about the Spirit's role versus the law's role can increase our ability to see His work in our lives daily. The Spirit can show us the harm of our behavior, and He can give us the resolve and power to overcome unloving actions. When we understand the consequences of our failures, the Spirit can provide us with the power to commit to responding in truth and love despite the circumstances. He guides us even in our darkest times, praying for us when we are unable (Rom. 8:26–27).

A recent event in my life is the best way for me to illustrate the complexity of walking with the Spirit.

Covid closed our little church in 2020. Shortly after we reopened, our pastor abruptly informed the congregation he was retiring. I had served at the church under his leadership for seventeen years, and it was quite a shock to our church and myself. All kinds of scenarios were floating around in my head. Since I had been volunteering as the youth pastor for all these years, should I try and step up to be the interim pastor? I didn't know what was best, and the pastor had not stuck around to solve any of these issues.

I decided to seek to become the temporary pastor. The Spirit was teaching me intensely about love and grace then, and I believed I could use this message to hold the church together. Even though I thought I was the right person for the job, it seemed like something other than what the Spirit wanted in this situation. Unfortunately, we had to leave the church and, with great sadness, watch it spiral to destruction. Friends became enemies and people left the church for good. All my efforts seemed to have failed.

God had a different plan for me. Since I was not called to be the interim pastor, and my business was slow, I felt led to invest in real estate. I wanted my business to be different and in order to achieve that I sought to avoid using the world's business model of success. Instead, my model would be to seek truth and love, guided by the Spirit, first and foremost in all my encounters and deals.

While I set out to discover everything I could about where to invest, I also made it my goal to seek the Spirit's help and to love everyone I encountered with His love. That meant not being overly concerned about getting the greatest deal or finding the best person to do the job. It meant making love a priority over success. Most importantly, I prayed about everything and trusting God for the results. As I responded in love when troubles came and trusted what the Spirit was doing, God grew me tremendously. My venture was not only successful, but more importantly, I loved everyone with Jesus' love. I was living by the Spirit.

Living by the Spirit looks similar to what Paul wrote to the Philippians:

> Rejoice in the Lord always. Again, I say, rejoice! Let everyone see your gentleness. The Lord is near! Do not be anxious about anything. Instead, in every situation, through prayer and petition with thanksgiving, tell your requests to God. And the peace of God that surpasses all understanding will guard your hearts and minds in Christ Jesus.
>
> Philippians 4:4-7 (NET)

Living by the Spirit is a different way of life. Instead of living driven by success or other self-aggrandizing motives, we are guided by the Spirit, who enables us to have faith, hope, and love in every circumstance.

Truly living by the Spirit will change us into a good person, but how is a good person defined? Society labels a person as good if they have learned to perform morally and socially acceptable ways of getting their needs fulfilled. With this definition, it is easy for secular society to label some Christians as bad and some non-Christians as good. Religious leaders may object to this labeling and want to be more specific, insisting a good person is defined by how they behave according to biblical norms and how they display their relationship with God. As I have pointed out, this definition also is misguided because it leads its followers into thinking they are good because of religious works they accomplish.

It is common to see Christians first embracing religious rules as the source of their goodness and then looking to the Spirit to help them fulfill the instructed terms of righteousness. This is unfortunate because religious laws and practices can be a roadblock that diverts believers from the Spirit's ministry in their hearts and takes them in the wrong direction. It focuses followers on how to function by standards of achievement to be good rather than being directed on how to love by the Spirit.

There is another challenge to our understanding of the source of our goodness. As followers of Jesus, we may agree that our relationship with God and abundant *good life* comes from living by the Spirit. However, watching people live successful lives without knowing or depending on the Spirit can be confusing. Both living by the flesh and following a religion can provide a way to overcome weaknesses and provide a path to success, but not without instilling harmful and ill-placed pride in our abilities and accomplishments.

If we purpose in our hearts to overcome weakness, and it works, do we then judge others who have not overcome the same weakness? A good example is when someone decides to lose weight and get into shape. If they succeed, they experience pride in their accomplishment; if they fail, they walk away dejected.

We may also fall into the trap of assuming other people are lazy mistake-makers when they can't reach our level of accomplishment. In our success, we can quickly forget that everyone has different strengths and weaknesses and that we can all fall short at times. Failure to acknowledge the truth about our shortcomings can cause us to judge and have no patience with others.

I am not making light of the existential conflict the command to live by the Spirit presents. Even if we turn to the Spirit for the big tasks in our lives, we still appear to accomplish the majority of our everyday smaller life tasks in our fleshly strength, seemingly without the Spirit. Do we need the Spirit to do things like brush our teeth? If we look at the mundane, knowing our abilities and resources come from God and that others do not necessarily share the same blessings and benefits, we then see the simplest things from a humble and thankful perspective. This understanding helps us live by the Spirit in even the most minor areas.

When we allow the Spirit to lead us, a renewing miracle of love occurs in our lives concerning judgment and pride. We embrace ourselves as "a new creation; old things ...passed away; behold all things have become new" (2 Cor. 5:17, NKJV). We are freed to succeed in the power of the Spirit as we grow in love. We all can experience this newness of life if we transition to living by the Spirit and away from accomplishments according to the desires and methods of flesh. The miracle of living by the Spirit and the love of the cross is that when we succeed, it does not lend us to judging more—it motivates us to love more.

The Spirit teaches us by guiding us in our daily situations without condemning obligations. We seek His guidance on what is true and loving when we discern between difficult circumstances. We also look for His prompting to love others in our commonplace interactions. Our ability to love grows daily as the Spirit leads us to love more. As we mature in love, our propensity to exhibit and live by prideful judgment and selfish ambition diminishes (1 John 4:15-21).

One may say, "I am not religious, and I certainly don't have 'prideful judgment and selfish ambition;' I merely follow the rules spelled out for us in the New Testament." In this approach, a person makes the mistake of interpreting New Testament passages as prescriptive passages, giving us new rules to live by—when they are meant to describe what the new life in the Spirit looks like.

This is best illustrated by "the fruit of the Spirit" in Galatians 5:22 (NET). It is a descriptive list of results of the Spirit's work in us, not a prescriptive list of characteristics for Christians to work on. Passages like these are tools to let us know when we are getting it right. Paul also lets us know when we are getting it wrong, as in the "works of the flesh"—a result of not living by the Spirit and living by either sin or rules to drive our lives. (Gal. 5:19, NET) Taking a descriptive, instead of a prescriptive, approach to perceived lists of rules in the New Testament is consistent with living "by the Spirit" so we "will not carry out the desires of the flesh" (Gal. 5:16, NET).

True goodness, for a believer, is a higher bar of goodness than obedience to rules and practices that are accomplished in one's own strength. It is the Spirit teaching us to love that transforms us into a good person (1 John 2:27). We can know we are on the right path to a *good life* when we recognize the true source of goodness comes from a belief in Jesus and living a life of love, guided by the Spirit.

A life of freedom in the Spirit is not avoiding the rules of the world, which we are obligated to obey; it is knowing that the rules do not own and control us. As God's children, we are free, although we do not use our freedom to indulge in whatever behavior we want. We use our freedom to put the truth of God and His love not only first but also above all else.

With no possibility of judgment or condemnation by law and being bathed in God's unconditional and immense love, we are free to listen to the Spirit and make whatever decision we need to. It is interesting that in our expanse of freedom, led by the Spirit, we make much better decisions than when we are chained to past failures and future fears.

Jesus said to Nicodemus, "The wind blows wherever it will, and you hear the sound it makes, but do not know where it comes from and where it is going. So it is with everyone who is born of the Spirit" (John 3:8, NET). Complete freedom in Christ, as we live by the Spirit, is an amazing state to strive for. We experience freedom differently than ever before because "if the Son sets you free, you will be really free" (John 8:36, NET).

Considering the freedom, love, and grace He has lavished us with, choosing to love ourselves and others in the power of the Spirit and not indulge our flesh should be easy, but unfortunately, it can still be a struggle. We live in an environment filled with suffering, which tries our faith, and we are constantly presented with delightful temptations for the flesh. We may sometimes feel we have one foot in the temporal world, which values achievement and following rules, and one foot in the eternal world of the Spirit, where His love in us brings our sanctification. Our dual citizenship makes walking in the light difficult, and we can often fail to demonstrate His love. The darkness of following the law—or rebelling against the law—can start to control us, leading us to give in to the desires of the flesh. In the face of our failures, we may forget all our successes and progress in putting on God's love. We may be tempted to turn back to a life of sin or enticed to live by rules and religion and abandon living out His way of love by the Spirit.

Thankfully, God's Spirit will never fail us. The Bible states plainly we will struggle, but God will grow us through our struggles. "For our struggle is not against flesh and blood, but against the rulers, against the powers, against the world rulers of this darkness, against the spiritual forces of evil in the heavens" (Eph. 6:12, NET). In our struggle, we must not fear what can kill the body but fear what can kill the soul, the part that will continue with us into eternity (Matt. 10:28). It is not a struggle in which we lose our place with God, but a struggle for what we will be like when we go to be with Him.

A journey with the Spirit is a struggle to be the honest, kind, and loving version of ourselves that God has already declared us to be. The way of the Spirit is infinitely better than sanctification achieved by our strength and guided by religious obligations and rules. It is a life lived by faith as we walk in the way of the cross. The Spirit teaches us to live cross-type love in our earthly state, and in doing so, we emulate our heavenly spiritual state, which we received at salvation.

When we live a life guided by the Spirit's love, He does most of the restoring, and we do very little. What is the little we must do? First, we must believe in and follow Jesus. Then, at the very least, we must choose to listen to the Spirit. There is still more we can do to be involved in our sanctification: we make time to meet with God, choose to seek love over the law, and decide not to judge by the law but to emulate Christ's grace and love. Even though we play a part in our transformation, what actually changes us is the truth and love poured into our hearts by the Spirit. It is made available when we begin to walk this new life with Him (Rom. 5:5; John 14:16-17).

Walking in the Spirit's love will bring true success in this life. True success is not even close to what the world deems as success. A truly fulfilled life comes from growing in love, sharing God's love, and knowing the truth as best we can. Success grows with hope, endures with faith, and is demonstrated by love. These virtues are achieved when people truly know their relationships with God, others, and themselves are what matters most. The highest success is reached when we are so overwhelmed by the love of God that we realize no sacrifice is too great in order to have God's love and share it with others.

God's Spirit in us enables this success, bringing "love, joy, peace, patience, kindness, goodness, faithfulness, gentleness, and self-control" into our lives (Gal. 5:22–23, NET). Our experience of these gifts often occurs while sacrificing for the sake of loving others. We are to "count it all joy" as we grow from suffering (Jas. 1:2, NKJV). Through suffering, our faith in Christ increases and our love for God, others, and ourselves grows as we walk by the Spirit. This lifelong journey is to be perfected in God's love demonstrated on the cross. Whether in ease or struggle, it brings our transformation from a life lived by the "desires of the flesh" to a life "led by the Spirit" and exhibiting His fruits (Gal. 5:16, 19, NASB). This is the essence of the *good life*––a life turned *love-side-up*.

Chapter 8: Getting on the Right Road

And we know that in all things God works for the good of those who love him, who have been called according to his purpose.

Romans 8:28 (NIV)

ALLOWING THE FATHER to transform our kingdom with His purpose is no easy task because it consists of a life lived with the love of the cross. It took me forty-five years to listen to what the Spirit was trying to teach me all my life. He implored me to embrace the love and sacrifice Jesus demonstrated on the cross—where He took away my sins, freed me from the law, and transforms me by teaching me to love. He showed me that this life is not about becoming righteous by following rules; instead, it is a process of the Spirit perfecting His children in heavenly love. God has unending truths to teach us no matter how long it takes, and He is faithful in teaching us through His Spirit.

My journey with God throughout my life, including my experiences in ministry, has been an incredible transformation, but not an easy one. Looking back, it is clear God reached out to me at a young age and walked me through the turmoil of my childhood. I had some wonderful friends, caring siblings, and an abundance of great Christian influences in my life. God even gave me experiences that were supernatural at times. The difficult times of abuse, sin, and hardships were also an unfortunate part of my experience. To make matters worse, I was often guilty of self-sabotage because I felt my efforts were rarely enough, leading to failure or underperforming. At times, the harder I tried, the harder I fell. Gratefully, God took my eclectic life of good and evil, along with my many failures and scattered successes, and He used them all to help me see life from a unique perspective regarding religion, faith, and His grace.

Discovering the *good life* found in Jesus did not come easy. I was never taught the way of love, lived by the Spirit. A glimpse of my journey will demonstrate how God helped me understand this aspect of His gospel.

By my seventeenth year, I fully embraced the need for Jesus, but it was not an easy road. My interaction with Christianity started very young, and my personal Christian struggle emerged in my heart around the age of twelve.

I grew up in a small town in the West as a backsliding conservative Christian. Our chaotic and dysfunctional family included three brothers and five sisters. The turmoil of my childhood and the hypocrisy of my father's faith led me to question what I wanted God's role to be in my kingdom. My father wore out Bibles from reading them every night, had us in church on Sunday, and brutally fought with my mother every Sunday afternoon. To solve some of the incongruencies of his Christianity, I found myself seeking explanations for life beyond the oversimplified and superficial Christian explanations. The standard answers I encountered did not adequately explain my situation, and that gave a foothold to my rebellion against my family and God. Throughout my waywardness Jesus continued to pursue me, and at sixteen, I began to see His importance in my life.

I drew closer to Jesus but struggled with knowing Him and experiencing His promised freedom and love. I knew plenty of commendable Christian people for whom the Christian religion of rules and confession seemed to inspire them to live somewhat honorable lives—especially on the outside—but it did not work for me. On the inside, my loneliness, anger, and judgment ran deep and continued to plague me. I found no religious cure. I had not been shown by my family how to behave appropriately. My behavior was acceptable but usually not exceptional, and I made some serious mistakes that hurt others. There was no Bible verse or repenting of sins that could fix me—no list I could follow, commitment I could make, or self-punishment I could inflict to change my behavior. Christianity had been a part of my life since day one, and it had not cured me of my problems. How could something so true not transform my life as I thought it would?

The route that led me to understand a life lived with the love of the cross as a solution to my problems started in high school. As a senior, I had a revival in my Christian life and made a plan to conquer my sin. I went through the New Testament and composed a list of all the sins to avoid and all the righteous actions I needed to perform. Wow! Now, that was a great list. There are few propositions we encounter in life that can make us feel more overwhelmed than a list of dos and don'ts, but I was up for the challenge. I thought I was doing well as I sought God with all my heart, avoided all the usual sins, respected my parents, loved my siblings, and even kept my actions respectable with my girlfriend. Because my behavior had been the opposite just a year prior, I felt I was a satisfactory Christian seeking the best way to include God in my kingdom.

The summer after my senior year of high school I had the privilege to be a camp counselor for six weeks. This was a fantastic experience of friendship, worship, and godly teaching. At the end of the season, the director provided a personal evaluation of each counselor. Now came the first significant blow to my legalism and self-empowered righteousness. The director said I was "not committed to God enough." As a young, idealistic Christian who had turned from a life of sin, I was crushed. At that moment, I broke the command not to hate. The harsh criticism from a Christian leader discouraged me. I was shaken in my resolve to be a good Christian. I found myself still committed to God, but my commitment to righteous behavior began to waver with this blow.

My first year of college at a Christian university catapulted me along on my journey of learning truths about Christianity and life. I was thoroughly engaged and enlightened as a young believer. Two of my favorite classes were "Developing a Christian Worldview," which helped me relate Christianity to the broader world, and "Introduction to Psychology," which helped me relate the truth of the Bible to my behavior. I seemed to be growing in a good direction; still, on the not-so-positive side, I began to question moral boundaries. I found myself seeking relationships with women as the answer to fill the deficit of love left by my broken family.

My sophomore year took a darker turn. I crossed moral lines in my dating relationship, which challenged my new Christian worldview. I was now a walking, living hypocrite. Not only was this against the rules of the college, but it was also a tremendous mental and moral conflict for someone headed into ministry. Through the Christian knowledge I gained, I could describe the Christian influence on Western culture, understand the Trinity, argue predestination, and explain the five points of Calvinism. Still, these truths did not help me control my daily behavior. Something needed to be fixed and learning more about Christianity and its rules did not solve my problems.

I held on to my legalistic regimen without alternative solutions guiding me. I committed to behaving better because I wanted to please God and work in ministry. This attempt to pull myself up by my bootstraps was a form of legalism as I sought to earn God's favor by behaving well in my own strength. Even though I knew God loved me when I failed, I still thought it was my job to behave better, crashing hard when I felt like I had let Him down. I did not fully understand that the process of the Spirit changing my heart was as important as changing my behavior.

I struggled throughout my twenties, wondering the same thoughts most people have: What is my purpose? Will I ever find a mate? Am I a good Christian even though I have sinned and still seem to fail quite often? Why is my life not easier? In the stew of my conscious and subconscious mind, these questions mingled with my feelings of loneliness, hurt, pride, disappointment, happiness, depression, and fleshly desires. My psychological health was a mess. I was attempting to get it right, yet I was far from finding out what "right" was. Not understanding how much I needed the guidance of God's Spirit, I did whatever I thought would improve my life as I constructed my kingdom.

I finished my youth ministry undergraduate program and interned at a church at twenty-two. The elders offered me a part-time junior high youth pastor position for $700 monthly. This was too little to live on, even in 1990, so I waited tables on the side to pay the bills. Feeling out of place and unappreciated, I went to my pastor for counseling and direction. He shared his opinion that I needed to go to seminary—the last place I wanted to go. I knew subconsciously that learning more about Christianity would not cure the confusion in my heart.

Instead of staying and following the pastor's direction, I left to look for another ministry. I found work in a structurally rigid environment as a counselor at a Christian wilderness therapy camp for troubled teens. It was a lonely, disciplined year of my life spent in the woods with delinquent kids. Although the structure was something I needed, isolation from peers at such a young age was more than I could handle.

I found myself back in Denver and began working as an electrician to make ends meet. My electrical skills advanced, but my heart was still set on the idea of doing ministry. Finally, listening to my old pastor's advice, I enrolled in seminary. After starting with night courses in the first term, I needed to increase to all-day Monday classes for the upcoming semester. The prospect of only working four days a week did not sit well with my electrical boss, who demanded I choose one or the other. I decided to drop seminary. My real boss, God, disagreed with my decision.

As I drove to work on the day seminary registration was to take place, a song blared on the Christian radio station with lyrics to the effect of, "How can you turn your back on me after what I've done for you?" I was slightly disconcerted by how applicable the song felt to my decision not to stay in seminary. When I arrived at the job site, no supervisor was present to instruct me on what to do, which had never happened before. I went to a payphone and called in. The voice on the other line instructed me to wait for the supervisor to show up. Sitting at a random job site for almost two hours with nothing to do gave me the impression that this was somehow God's hand at work. Agonizing over my decision to quit seminary, as the time ticked away on my watch, I realized it was still not too late to register if I left right then. Finally, I followed God's obvious prompting, quit my job on the spot, and went to enroll. I felt God step into my life that day and I was high on the Spirit. Seminary was right where God wanted me.

It is intriguing how God subtly works in our lives, and we struggle to see it until we take the time to observe what He has done and is doing. As I sought to seek God's will and purpose, my circumstances continued to improve. One life-changing improvement was meeting a fantastic woman shortly after graduating from seminary, and we were married two years later. We entered ministry together when I took a part-time junior high youth pastor position in Aurora, Colorado. God began to bless me with a family, a church, and a budding business, all at the same time.

At thirty-four, I stepped away from that ministry, not knowing it would be my last time working officially in a church. The three years spent at the church was a life-changing experience, and we parted with fond feelings about what we had accomplished. Ministry was not over for us by any means. We began volunteering at a church near our house on the west side of Denver, helping another youth pastor acquaintance. I loved working with youth, whether paid or not.

A painful experience at this ministry made me question everything I knew about the church and what it meant to follow Jesus. Volunteering as a youth leader was enjoyable and fruitful for the first year, and the youth pastor and I became relatively close friends. The church pressured him to increase numbers and morale in my second year there. My wife and I began investing more time and energy in helping, which proved futile. Unfortunately, the church leadership had already decided about the youth group's health. They then hired a consultant to evaluate the youth program and enact change. The consultant looked past all of our progress and saw only the weaknesses. A portion of the blame for the failing youth group was laid on me because I helped with many aspects of the ministry.

Things got even worse. The consultant, also a close friend of mine, called me one night trying to confirm his suspicion that I wanted to take over the youth group. Since it was not my intention and he got nowhere in the conversation, he came right out and said, "Ernie, you're a washed-up youth pastor trying to take over John's job." This statement from my friend tore out all my desire to be a part of this ministry or any ministry in the future. It hurt to the core because I was giving everything to this group and God, and I was pinned as the problem, told I was a failure, and accused of trying to stab my friend in the back. I tried to ignore the hurtful, wrong accusations and even continued to help until the church ended my friend's job, but the hurt did not go away. It ripped at my heart, and each little incident brought it back. I was baffled about what God wanted from me and why He would do this to me through His pastor and my friend. I felt I had failed God and was finished with the ministry, thinking: *"What other sign could God give me?"* I felt as if God had hit me in the head with a big stick, not to correct me but to knock me out.

Shortly after the experience, I began to avoid reading the Bible. I knew I could not perfectly obey even one of the commandments. I had studied God's Word my whole life, and I certainly had enough Scripture to remind me of my inadequacy. I also knew the Bible well enough to keep up with my youth group teaching. I continued to devote myself to work and to my wife and kids, feeling depressed whenever I let anyone down. Since I believed I had failed God as a youth worker, I wanted to get this part of my life right. Even with all my efforts, I was not always successful. I was relatively happy—except when someone expected what I could not deliver or people were dissatisfied with my work. I tried not to let either happen.

God was not through with me. In my time of struggle, I stumbled on a radio show by Aaron Budjen with Living God Ministries.[8] Jesus changed my life through Aaron's teaching about the complete forgiveness given at the cross and expanded my understanding of the gospel. My eyes were slowly opened through listening to countless hours of his broadcasts. I finally understood God's great forgiveness and how He gives us His Spirit and frees us from the law. What a life-changing realization! I understood it was God's plan for me to back off Scripture to allow God to correct my misconceptions about salvation and His grace. When I dove back into studying the Bible, I began to see how Christ's work on the cross played a central role in how I was to build my kingdom.

This is not an expression of disappointment about my ministry path because I can see that God took me on a journey to a place I would have never gone if I had stayed in full-time ministry. The small mountain church, where I attended and pastored the youth during this time, was a perfect environment for me to process this transition. I did not abandon God, nor did He abandon me, our relationship grew closer and deeper through all of my struggles.

Even though I approached my growth process slightly differently than most, many have had a similar experience of trying to understand precisely what God is doing in their lives. We can look back and make assessments about the life we have lived and can see God's hand in multiple places. Our lives are often built clumsily in the dark, especially when building our kingdom without God. But we should not be without hope because we know God takes our mistakes and shapes them into something that can benefit us.

If, like me, you can get a glimpse of your freedom from the law and take hold of the love Jesus demonstrated on the cross, it will transform how you read Scripture and transform how you interact with others. You can know that the creator God, Jesus Christ, has chosen you. He loves you, He died for you, and He has given you an abundance of gifts. As you understand these truths, your world will be opened to His transformation. Jesus has shared His glory with us and established a place for each of us in His kingdom. When we learn to live the love of the cross in our lives and begin seeking His kingdom and not our own, the Spirit is free to accomplish things in us and through us that we have not dared to dream of.

Chapter 9: Starting with the Essentials

Continue working out your salvation with awe and reverence, for the one bringing forth in you both the desire and the effort – for the sake of his good pleasure – is God.

Philippians 2:12–13 (NET)

TO UNDERSTAND HOW SALVATION sets us on a whole new journey toward a *good life*, we need to explore a basic understanding of what following Jesus entails and how it impacts our lives. I will describe the essentials from two perspectives: the intellectual and the experiential.

The Intellectual Perspective

We often come to Jesus thinking He will solve all our problems. We envision He will set up His kingdom in our lives, making things copacetic, yet we still have the daunting potential to cause destruction through foolish mistakes and willfully doing evil against God, ourselves, and others. We are weak, broken, and at times even deny Christ. Although God does meaningful work in us, our dysfunction and problems persist.

We may have imagined we would eventually be able to overcome sin as we grew closer to God. We quickly realize this is not the case because conquering sin is an inhuman proposition. It is important to know that this common struggle with sin does not demonstrate a lack of positive growth. Learning to live with the temptation of sin is a big piece of the puzzle which helps us to see the whole picture of the change Jesus brings.

Let's begin with some basics concerning how we are transformed at salvation. When we think of ourselves as transformed, what does that mean? What does the term, self, even refer to? According to the words of Jesus, written down by Mark, human selves are comprised of four parts: "heart," "soul," "mind," and "strength" (Mark 12:30, NASB1995). The "heart" can be described as one's center motive source.[9] The "soul" is the part of the person that will live eternally.[10] The "mind" consists of our thoughts, desires, and feelings, which will also be a part of our eternity.[11] "Strength" is bodily force and might.[12]

In other places in Scripture, the writers seem to embrace the idea of humans as two parts instead of four. As two parts, one might describe the heart and the soul as the immortal part, referred to as spirit, and the mind and strength as the material part, referred to as flesh. There is a caveat: while our person is immortal, the brain is not. The word mind can overlap as a reference to our immortal person and not merely refer to the brain. The brain appears to function as the organ that connects our immaterial self, our spirit, with our material self or the flesh. The flesh consists of our brain and body. The flesh is the part of us that behaves most like an animal and can cause our habits, desires, and thought patterns.

Before we were Christians, our spirits were dead in relation to our connection to God, and we were ruled by the flesh. When we are saved, our spirit is made alive, and we attempt to put to death the things of the flesh (Rom. 8:13). We try to prevent the selfish desires of the flesh from controlling us. The Holy Spirit now indwells us and communes with our new living spirit. In this new life we live, sanctification is accomplished through God's Spirit leading our spirit, teaching us truth and love. As our spirit is transformed—the part of us which lives forever—we also seek to change our fleshly behavior to be wholly transformed.

As believers, we are not to live as the world lives. The term world refers to a system of meeting our fleshly needs and wants in ways contrary to the love of Jesus. Living as the world lives can involve seeking success, affirmation, power, and control at the expense of others, wanting and taking more than we need, and putting ourselves first. It can also be characterized by someone seeking safety and comfort over doing acts of love. We are to be in the world, but we are not to love the world (1 John 2:15–17).

As Christians, we can be tested by Satan, who is a fallen angel that has an agenda to thwart God's plan. Satan, along with his fellow workers, attempts to lead us to live as slaves to our flesh and to the world so he can be in control. We do not need to fear Satan, his demons, or the world because the Father gives us the ability to conquer them (1 John 5:4–5).

We don't conquer the world alone but with the power of the Holy Spirit. He is the third person of the godhead who indwells us and guides us in love and truth. Truth is the knowledge of how the world works and an understanding of how God interacts with us in that world. The flesh, the world, and Satan have no power to control us as we live to love as Jesus loved, in the power of the Spirit.

When we are redeemed, sin, in the sense of an action we take, is given a whole new meaning. Sin is now a state in which we give in to the flesh, the world, or Satan and commit regrettable acts which are the opposite of love. Sin can be more simply understood as unbelief in Jesus (for the non-Christian) and failure to love as the Spirit leads (for the believer).

Upon our confession of belief, we receive the gift of God's forgiveness for our sins. No matter how much we sinned in the past, we can let go of our failures and start over with the condemnation for our sins removed. Subsequently, we are freed from our guilt and shame. His forgiveness also applies to any future sins we may commit.

When we become God's children, His love is lavished on us. He now accepts us and desires to be with us. His love is demonstrated by God wanting to know and experience who we are. God's love is unconditional, and we cannot do anything to change His love for us. It was chiseled on His body at the cross; He has the markings of love which cannot be removed.

We grow closer to God by exercising our faith in Him. Faith is a decision to acknowledge and believe in God and what He has done. In faith, we set aside our old self, who was a slave to the flesh, the world, Satan, and sin, and we choose to walk by the Spirit in God's love, truth, and forgiveness. Walking by faith, we discover our new self, which has been given an abundant *good life* we did not know was possible in our old self. Through faith, we begin to discover His new purpose for us and the new self He intended us to be.

We are changed as believers by walking in the Spirit by faith, living to love, and seeking the truth—especially about who we are in God and how loved we are by Him. Although we are not changed overnight, it does not mean we do not change. When we choose to believe and experience Christ, we enter a new growth process of life known as sanctification. Through sanctification, the Spirit grows us away from our slavery to sin and fear, and He grows us toward God's love as His children. God moves in each follower's life according to His purpose. In the midst of our journey, it is often hard to see where He is taking us, but we trust it is a good place.

The Experiential Perspective

All I have just written about the intellectual elements of salvation is a lot to take in and understand. While the truths of our salvation help us to know what and why we believe and direct us in the true way of the cross, experiencing salvation is just as important. When I was young, I often wondered why Jesus did not sustain me with a plethora of supernatural experiences to bolster my faith. Thankfully, I knew the verse, "You shall not tempt the Lord your God" (Matt. 4:7, NKJV), which restrained me from attempting to force Him to manifest His presence. Although we cannot force God to perform miracles, they do happen to all of us. If we can recognize them, they will become a vital part of our Christian journey. As we look back at the past, sometimes we can clearly see the supernatural in the circumstances God orchestrates.

As a young man, God manifested His unique presence to me on several occasions. I remember a specific experience in 1984: attending a Bill Gothard seminar for teens at McNichols Sports Arena in Denver, Colorado. We sang hymns, a cappella style, in a packed event with more than ten thousand people. As we sang, our voices resonated, causing the whole building to vibrate and shake. It was a fantastic experience that displayed the sense of the supernatural. I later went to other concerts in that arena, including the U2 concert, "Rattle and Hum," but there was never again a rattle and hum like the one I felt while singing hymns as a junior in high school.

Earlier that year, my father invited me to a Mike Warnke Christian comedy show. While Warnke had some disheartening personal problems, God still used him to preach a powerful message about His love for us. The supernatural love of Jesus filled my heart that night, which made me aware of the destructive path I was on. My friend's older sister, who was not a Christian, attended with me, and she too felt God's supernatural love overwhelm her. For the previous couple of months, we had both lived enslaved to our chosen vices, mostly involving sex and drugs. We both left the arena crying and praising God for the love He showed us. In my life, God touched me through this broken man, and it profoundly changed me.

My close friend from high school followed Jesus but was still in and out of trouble his whole adult life. Even though he went forward at a Billy Graham crusade, his lifestyle did not change. However, his faith gave him a place to turn for help, and Jesus was there for him as he continued to struggle with his destructive behavior. As a result of the life he lived, he died at the young age of thirty-five, which troubled me because I had a strong premonition that I would die at that very age. I even had slight anxiety as I approached my birthday. I now understand that my mysterious thoughts were related to my high school friend, with whom I lived my wayward years. If I had not allowed the love of Jesus to change my life, I most likely would be lying there with him in the grave.

Even if God saves us from an accident, do we give Him credit? I rolled my Jeep down an embankment—three complete rollovers at sixty-five miles per hour with no seat belt—and survived it with barely a scratch. Did God save me from severe injury or even death in that accident? The answer is "yes," but can I prove it? I can look back on several life events and say God most likely spared my life, guided me, and opened and closed doors.

Moses was eighty years old when he encountered God at the burning bush (Exod. 3:1–6). This is a good reminder that it is never too late to step into God's plan. After years of struggling and wandering, God called Moses to do a great task. He was entering retirement age and likely needed a physical crutch like his staff. God knew he also needed a spiritual crutch for the task He was calling him to do. He gave Moses the burning bush experience and a staff with which he could exhibit the power of God (Exod. 4:1–5). Moses was drastically changed in a moment from a misguided shepherd to a prophet who would change the world.

God supernaturally interacts with each of us by a means He determines is right on an individual basis. For some, it is a still, small voice; others see miracles. Blaise Pascal, the great French mathematician and scientist, wrote of his supernatural encounter with God, which was found sewn in his coat pocket after his death:

The year of grace 1654,

Monday, 23 November,

…From about half past ten at night until about half past midnight,

FIRE.

GOD of Abraham, GOD of Isaac, GOD of Jacob

not of the philosophers and of the learned.

Certitude. Certitude. Feeling. Joy. Peace.

GOD of Jesus Christ.

My God and your God.

Your GOD will be my God.

Forgetfulness of the world and of everything, except GOD.

He is only found by the ways taught in the Gospel.

Grandeur of the human soul.

Righteous Father, the world has not known you, but I have known you.

Joy, joy, joy, tears of joy.

I have departed from him:

They have forsaken me, the fount of living water.

My God, will you leave me?

Let me not be separated from him forever.

This is eternal life, that they know you, the one true God, and the one that you sent, Jesus Christ.

Jesus Christ.

Jesus Christ.

I left him; I fled him, renounced, crucified.

Let me never be separated from him.

He is only kept securely by the ways taught in the Gospel:

Renunciation, total and sweet.

Complete submission to Jesus Christ and to my director.

Eternally in joy for a day's exercise on the earth.

May I not forget your words. Amen.[13]

This testimonial poem of Pascal's other-worldly experience is an inspiring example of a supernatural encounter with Jesus Christ. It is not something we are accustomed to hearing from a highly educated and accomplished person. This type of experience is essential for faith because our mind and reason can trick and fail us. It appears Pascal was aware of this weakness and therefore always kept this reminder of God's conversation with him on his person.

I look for the supernatural presence of Jesus in my daily life in various ways. He guides me to love in the smallest of circumstances. While singing praise songs, God has made me aware of His felt presence. Meditation often gives me alertness to His Spirit in me. For several months in my late twenties, while I meditated, I entered into a surreal awareness of His presence and longed to stay there. As these experiences happened, I felt so full I believed I could do extraordinary feats for God. I was willing to go to the most challenging and loneliest places for Him if only I continually experienced this level of His presence.

At times we may proclaim we want to encounter God in a spectacular supernatural manner, but I am not sure we can handle the impact on our lives. Our actions from that point on would need to reflect the gift given. Even Moses failed to respect God's presence when he struck the rock at Kadesh instead of speaking to it (Num. 20:1–13).

It appears it is safer for God to speak to us in a manner we can handle. In almost every conversion, God provides a subtle concrete experiential marker that can be the anchor that holds us steady in trying times. It is like the feeling of passionate love one initially has for one's mate. This love grows into companion love and then matures into committed love as partners mature and experience difficulties and successes. This matured love does not disregard the present reality, nor does it forget the initial events that began the marriage. A healthy relationship with God values the past but is not stuck there; it is living and vibrant daily.

Combining the Intellectual and the Experiential

Some may receive miracles to spur on their belief, but it is vital not to depend solely on those experiences for our faith. This can short-circuit the process of forming a firm belief based on a daily walk with God, including the hard grind of study, prayer, and faith lived by action. Constant supernatural intervention could become a crutch that hinders one from growing a deeper faith. Our beliefs are not sustained by one miraculous event but by the reality of the complete understanding of what we receive as we believe. A supernatural experience bolstering our belief can be as important as reason, but it should not stop there. As capable, we should seek to grow a faith that embraces the supernatural but also looks to reason and natural experience.

Many believers fail to recognize the most significant supernatural experience God gives us. It is when Jesus begins to manifest His love in us through the indwelling of the Spirit. This is one of God's great miracles in a believer's life, considering how hard it is to get anyone to change their mind or behavior—let alone both. God consistently transforms the lives of those who believe in and follow Jesus with His love, yet we seem to overlook its magnitude and importance.

Although we receive the riches of God's love at salvation (Rom. 12:2), a typical Christian may not fully experience this blessing. Many surrender selected parts of their lives and then wonder why God does not bless their whole life. It seems God will not give us what we need until we release what we are clutching onto as our worldly means of fulfilling our lives. Our many distractions block God's gift of love (Jas. 4:2–3). When we let go of the methods outside of God that we use to fulfill our needs and wants, and instead trust Christ to provide, He gives us more than we need in return.

Another deception about how our lives change is to think that salvation consists predominantly of physical blessings—especially the ones we think we want. Instead, He gives us His salvation that brings love and truth into our hearts which is the fulfillment we truly need (Jas. 2:5, 8; Rom. 5:8). We are not called to a kingdom of good works, power, influence, riches, or comfort but to a family of love (Matt. 6:24–34; Rom. 12:1–2; 1 Cor. 13; Phil. 2:1–8; John 18:36). At salvation, we become receivers of every good gift and blessing from God (Eph. 1:3), and we become members of His family in which nothing can separate us from His love (Rom. 8:14–17, 38–39; Gal. 4:6–7). We are His children because we choose to believe in Jesus, accept Him, and love Him in response to His choosing, accepting, and loving us. When we embrace God's kingdom of love and truth and disregard the world's vision of success, we progress toward a *good life* because how we look at the world changes.

As we grow in our new relationship with the Father, we seek to know Him, and He seeks to know us. We can rest in His kindness and love for us because this love never changes, even though He knows our every thought and deed. We share our needs with Him, understanding He has our best interest in mind (John 14:15–21). We rejoice that He has removed our moral debts, and we strive not to hold obligations nor harbor grudges toward others (Matt. 6:12; Rom. 13:8). We seek to love and not to judge, nor to do evil to others. We pray that God will protect us from others who would harm us (Matt. 6:13; Rom. 12:21). Lastly, we have peace and contentment knowing God is in control of all that happens, and He offers us a new life in a new kingdom (Rom. 8:26–39).

In this new life, Jesus offers hope for this new relationship with God:

> So then, if anyone is in Christ, he is a new creation; what is old has passed away – look, what is new has come! And all these things

are from God who reconciled us to himself through Christ, and who has given us the ministry of reconciliation. In other words, in Christ God was reconciling the world to himself, not counting people's trespasses against them, and he has given us the message of reconciliation.

Second Corinthians 5:17–19 (NET)

Jesus offers hope for the resolution of our past sins and a new life free of condemnation from sin (1 John 1:9, 3:20; 2 Cor. 5:17–19). Our separation from God has been removed and replaced by a ministry of forgiveness, love, and restored relationships.

In this new life, our motive for living changes. We live for a new king who commands us to give and sacrifice for others and not to live only for ourselves. "The thief comes only to steal and kill and destroy; I came that they may have life, and have it abundantly" (John 10:10, NASB). He came so that we can live a *good life*. We can live abundantly by the Spirit, in the love and truth He brings, or we can live life as the thief: stealing, killing, and destroying. Our lives can be extraordinary and good when we live by His Spirit (John 1:4, 10:10, 12:25; Rom. 8:2).

Seeking His kingdom, we are given the hope and the reality of the presence of Christ, both now and in the future. Even though we have a purpose and destiny in this life, it is a temporary season in our eternal life with Christ.

> In My Father's house are many mansions; if it were not so, I would have told you. I go to prepare a place for you. And if I go and prepare a place for you, I will come again and receive you to Myself; that where I am, there you may be also.

John 14:2–3 (NKJV)

Christ's Spirit dwells with us in this life, but this life is not all there is. Physical death for Christians is changing places from living with the Lord on Earth to living with the Lord in Heaven (John 5:24). Jesus is always with us, and He has prepared specific places and specific ways for us to be with Him in this life and the next (John 14:1–6.). Wherever Jesus is, we are with Him, and He is with us wherever we are. He desires to live and reign with us, and He hopes we desire to say yes to His invitation.

Chapter 10: The Navigator

And if the Spirit of him who raised Jesus from the dead is living in you, he who raised Christ from the dead will also give life to your mortal bodies because of his Spirit who lives in you. ...For those who are led by the Spirit of God are the children of God. The Spirit you received does not make you slaves, so that you live in fear again; rather, the Spirit you received brought about your adoption to sonship. And by him we cry, "Abba, Father." The Spirit himself testifies with our spirit that we are God's children.

Romans 8:11, 14–16 (NIV)

MY QUEST TO UNDERSTAND the Spirit started when I was a senior in high school. I wanted to understand and experience the supernatural presence of the Holy Spirit in a concrete way. I learned very little of Him from my Baptist church growing up but I did learn about Him from Charismatic churches that my mother preferred. They showed her love by not discriminating against her for being divorced. I sat through more than one sermon in which a preacher stated his car miraculously did not run out of gas even though the gauge read empty for untold miles. Sick and broken people came to the front of the church to be prayed for and then professed to be healed. I witnessed people speaking in tongues and being slain in the Spirit, although I did not experience either.

At times, I wondered if these miracles were authentic. I found myself even more confused when the pastor's wife died of cancer. Still, I begged God for a supernatural filling of the Spirit. I wanted confirmation God was real, to touch Him, and for Him to meet me in a unique way. I pleaded with Him for the gift of tongues, but I only received sounds that seemed a product of my own creation. All of it left me wondering more and more about how the Spirit interacts with us.

I was not wholly discouraged in my quest for God's presence. When I was about eighteen, two events in my life demonstrated He was there.

First, God healed my warts after my mother prayed for them. For years, I had unsightly warts on both hands. After having a doctor remove them, only to have them grow back several months later, I turned to my mom for prayer. Within a week, they were gone, never to return. I still have the scars to remind me where they resided. It was an amazing little blessing God used in my life.

The second was the "Happy Camper" van. I was accepted to be a counselor at Camp Bethel, the Bible camp I grew up attending. They asked local churches for a van to transport kids daily to the lake one mile from the camp. I was excited to volunteer our old green van and then went to the Lord in prayer. I prayed, "God if it is Your will, have my dad agree to use his old van. I have twenty dollars for the project; may You bless the twenty dollars and provide the material for seats." Strangely enough, my dad was excited about the idea too. We did not have a lot of money, so I wasn't sure that he would spare with the van. A friend of a friend was converting an old school bus to a camper. I was able to obtain the seat frames for free and use them with only a little modification. I still needed bottoms, backs, and cushions. I used ten dollars to purchase a sheet of plywood and a bit of hardware, which was just enough board to cut up for the seats and back rests. My parents had an old foam mattress that worked perfectly for cushions, but what would I cover them with? We lived in a small-town of 1500 people, still, yet I sensed God telling me I would find the material at a yard sale. At the first sale I stopped, there were two rolls of orange and one roll of black seat covering material, which I bought for ten dollars. After stitching the covers and assembling the seats in the van, for the small sum of twenty dollars, the Holy Spirit and I fitted the van for twenty kids. The final touch was to paint "Happy Campers" on the side in gold. It was a rewarding project where I saw God's hand at each step of the way. This simple experience tremendously bolstered my belief in the Spirit who was with me.

These were not my only experiences, and as I grew older, I continued to wonder about the Holy Spirit, seek Him, and even find Him supernaturally on occasion. I am convinced He is with me, and I understand more and more why He does not continually make His presence known in an overwhelmingly supernatural way. It may be that if we are given too many supernatural experiences by the Spirit, it would be difficult to exist in the normal struggles of the natural world.

Humans are weak and are easily tempted to lean too heavily on the spectacular. How quickly would we begin to use our special revelation to have unsubstantiated confidence and influence over others? Simon, an old sorcerer, and a new Christian, wanted to buy the gift of "the laying on of hands" Peter and John possessed (Acts 8:18–19). He envied the power it would give him and most likely would have abused it. A supernatural gift of the Spirit is like any gift God gives, including love. These gifts can be used for godly purposes but can be misused as well. Although a supernatural encounter with the Spirit is what we think we want, it can be challenging to know how to respond when experiencing it. Even if we respond appropriately initially, we can still fall into the trap of pride and allow our hearts to be corrupted by power and influence.

Every believer is vulnerable to misusing the supernatural power of God. Think of the prophet Elisha. When a group of youth mocked him, he let out a curse, and forty-two of them were mauled by two bears (2 Kings 2:24). Even though the prophet Elisha was a man of God, it appears he misused his power. Another sad example is Peter's mistake when he presided over the death of Ananias and Sapphira, which brought fear to the church (Acts 4:32–5:11). This action is antithetical to the love and grace Jesus brought. Perhaps Peter thought he was restoring the kingdom of Israel to the earth through the church. We may think we want the power of the Spirit to perform miracles, but trusting the Spirit to participate in our lives in the way He sees fit, according to what we truly need, may be safer and more edifying.

My hesitancy towards a miracle-led life is not to say that I don't want the Spirit in me to do extraordinary things. When John the Baptist announced Jesus, he proclaimed that Jesus would baptize us with the Spirit (Matt. 3:11). Jesus later told His disciples that He would send them a comforter, referring to the Spirit coming to live in us (John 14:16–17, 15:26). Once saved, our bodies become the temple of the Holy Spirit (1 Cor. 6:19). The Spirit is the person of the Godhead who intermingles with our spirit and lives in us, teaching us truths, perfecting us in love, and comforting us (2 Tim. 1:7). God is in us, and we are in Him (1 John 4:16; John 14:20).

Consider this list of some of the profound claims about the Spirit made by Jesus, by the disciple John, and by the apostle Paul.

Jesus said the Spirit is our helper:

> But when the Helper comes, whom I shall send to you from the Father, the Spirit of truth who proceeds from the Father, He will testify of Me.
>
> John 15:26-27 (NKJV)

John preached the Spirit is our teacher:

> But the anointing which you have received from Him abides in you, and you do not need that anyone teach you; but as the same anointing teaches you concerning all things, and is true, and is not a lie, and just as it has taught you, you will abide in Him.
>
> First John 2:27 (NKJV)

Paul exhorted Timothy to seek the Spirit:

> Therefore I remind you to stir up the gift of God which is in you through the laying on of my hands. For God has not given us a spirit of fear, but of power and of love and of a sound mind.
>
> Second Timothy 1:6-7 (NKJV)

We are taught by the Spirit to love one another:

> But concerning brotherly love you have no need that I should write to you, for you yourselves are taught by God to love one another.
>
> First Thessalonians 4:9 (NKJV)

Living by the Spirit brings amazing transformation.

> But the fruit of the Spirit is love, joy, peace, longsuffering, kindness, goodness, faithfulness, gentleness, self-control. Against such there is no law.
>
> Galatians 5:22-23 (NKJV)

The Spirit gives us all unique gifts to build up the church body.

> But the manifestation of the Spirit is given to each one for the profit of all: for to one is given the word of wisdom through the Spirit, to another the word of knowledge through the same Spirit, to another faith by the same Spirit, to another gifts of healings by the same Spirit, to another the working of miracles, to another prophecy, to another discerning of spirits, to another different kinds of tongues, to another the interpretation of tongues. But one and the same Spirit works all these things, distributing to each one individually as He wills.
>
> First Corinthians 12:7-11 (NKJV)

Living with the gift of the Spirit is a whole new way of life. We walk with a comforter and guide who renews our souls and cares deeply about the predicaments and outcomes of our lives. He is the person of God within us, who helps us when we are weak and do not know what to pray. He intercedes to God on our behalf, especially when we do not have even a glimpse of the big picture:

> In the same way the Spirit also helps our weakness; for we do not know how to pray as we should, but the Spirit Himself intercedes for us with groanings too deep for words; and He who searches the hearts knows what the mind of the Spirit is, because He intercedes for the saints according to the will of God. And we know that God causes all things to work together for good to those who love God, to those who are called according to His

purpose. For those whom He foreknew, He also predestined to become conformed to the image of His Son, so that He would be the firstborn among many brethren; and these whom He predestined, He also called; and these whom He called, He also justified; and these whom He justified, He also glorified.

Romans 8:26–30 (NASB)

The Spirit plays a vital role in our lives and our choices as we grow with fellow believers. Lasting change does not come through our efforts; on the contrary, we are given the Holy Spirit to heal our past, embody our present, and give us hope for our future (Rom. 8:26). We begin to live a *good life* as our relationship with the Father grows through the indwelling of the Holy Spirit. Listening to the Spirit enlightens us in the truth, setting us free from the darkness of our old ways which controlled and enslaved us (Gal. 5:16). He gives us clarity to decipher the crazy mixture of wrong and right intentions that reside in our hearts (Rom. 7:19). Our new relationship with Him can bring a comfort that helps us to cope with the loneliness many of us feel (2 Cor. 1:3–5). His presence calms our fear of the unknown (Phil. 4:6–7), giving us a hope for the future (Rom. 12:1–2). He tells us we are infinitely valuable when we might see ourselves as worthless (John 8:10–11). He validates that our importance exists because of His love for us, freeing us from a worth based on things out of our control (John 3:16). Our lives are changed by the Holy Spirit and all the gifts He brings when He comes to indwell in us.

These blessings received from having the Spirit in us are overwhelming, and experientially they seem almost incomprehensible. We may struggle to see them and the transformational effect they have in our lives. When Paul says to "continue working out your salvation with awe and reverence" (Phil. 2:12, NET), this might confuse us as to who is doing the work in us, but he goes on to say, "For the one bringing forth in you both the desire and the effort—for the sake of his good pleasure—is God" (Phil. 2:13, NET). Paul encourages us to cooperate with the complicated transformation work the Spirit is completing inside us.

As we grow, we learn that this new life in the Spirit means walking with a destiny to display God's image as we were created to do in the beginning. He is the one who implements the Father's call for us, justifying us and giving us glory as God did for the saints in the past. The Spirit in us is the key to the Father working out His destiny with us and for us.

When we step out in faith, the Spirit is our power and motivation to love others as Christ loved. The Spirit interacts with us through a new law written on our hearts. He has a universal goal of truth and love and a specific purpose that God tailors to each individual (John 14:17, 26). With the Spirit, we work to be perfected in His love but each at our own pace, in our own ways, and at different stages (1 John 2:5, 4:12, 18). In the New Testament, we have a vague picture of what it looks like but, since it is a relationship between the Spirit and a unique individual, it can look different for each person (John 15:15).

This mysterious transforming power of the Holy Spirit changes us dramatically on the inside, yet He seems to do His work in a non-overwhelming way. He gives us the power to love and understand the world around us. He manifests loving character in our lives. He anoints us and teaches us truths, especially truths about His salvation and love. He comforts us, and He manifests His gifts in our lives to edify the body of Christ. The Christian life is not a self-help system; it is a supernatural journey with God, in which the Spirit of God enters us and performs miracles on whatever scale He sees fit.

Chapter 11: Turn at the Cross

For the message about the cross is foolishness to those who are perishing, but to us who are being saved it is the power of God.

I Corinthians 1:18 (NET)

UNDERSTANDING THE CROSS is key to understanding our life in Christ, our complete freedom from sin, the end of the law for those who believe, and the new way of love without condemnation. In addition, Christ on the cross models for us the ability to embrace our troubles for the sake of love. I will address these provisions of the cross in the coming chapters. They are all vital to finding the *good life* because they turn our lives *love-side-up*.

J.C. Ryle, a great theologian of late 1800's centered his ministry around the cross in much the same way I am advocating for.

> "The cross is the grand peculiarity of the Christian religion. Other religions have laws and moral precepts, forms and ceremonies, rewards and punishments. But other religions cannot tell us of a dying Savior. They cannot show us the cross. This is the crown and glory of the gospel. This is that special comfort that belongs to it alone. Miserable indeed is that religious teaching which calls itself Christian but contains nothing of the cross. A man who teaches in this way might as well profess to explain the solar system but tell his hearers nothing about the sun. The cross is the strength of a minister. I for one would not be without it for all the world. I would feel like a soldier without arms, an artist without his pencil, a pilot without his compass, or a laborer without his tools.

Let others, if they desire, preach the law and morality; let others hold forth the terrors of hell and the joys of heaven; let others drench their congregations with teachings about the sacraments and the church, but give me the cross of Christ. This is the only lever that has ever turned the world upside down and made men forsake their sins. And, if the preaching of the cross will not do this, nothing will."[14]

The cross was the defining moment in Jesus' ministry and life. Understanding the meaning and purpose of the cross and how intensely it demonstrates that God wants a relationship with us is foundational to the gospel. Christ's work on the cross—completing the covenant of the law—brought the possibility of the end of our separation from God and the end of the reign of sin and condemnation. To accomplish this, Christ bore our sins and suffered our deserved penalty of death in order to forgive us, to take away our sin, to take away the old covenant law, and to declare us righteous—worthy to be in His presence. His loving act on the cross is the gospel because it is the act that provided for our rebirth as new creations and a bridge to a loving relationship with the Father, making it possible for the re-indwelling of the Holy Spirit in us

The cross is the opposite of what humanity would expect from a savior. Our savior should be a knight in shining armor riding in on a white horse to conquer our enemies. Our savior should be strong and fix all our problems. Our savior should answer all our questions and give us solutions to the things that trouble us. Our savior should build a kingdom in the mold we see fit. The cross did not make sense—to the Jews, it was "a stumbling block, and to Gentiles foolishness" (1 Cor. 1:23, NASB1995)—why would a savior have to die?

To begin to understand the cross, it will be helpful to understand the concept of the shedding of blood to cover our sins. Throughout history, God has asked humans to do things that may seem strange to facilitate a relationship with Him. One of those things at odds with our modern minds, yet central to the Jewish religion, was the sacrifice of animals to cover their sins and to demonstrate their faith in God.

In today's world, a requirement to kill animals doesn't seem logically sensible for the benefit of a relationship. Contrary to that sentiment, in Christian and Jewish doctrines, the blood of an animal represents a covenant between two parties. An example is God's covenant with Abram in Genesis 15, where animals were slaughtered to establish the agreement. Similarly, Jesus referred to His blood as the new covenant between Himself and His followers (Matt. 26:28). His blood served as a symbol of the binding agreement Christians are asked to enter.

Animal sacrifice can also represent a harsh but poignant picture of the damage we cause when we break a relationship through our evil behavior. It can be understood as a substitutionary death for the death we deserve for our sins (Isa. 53:6, Matt. 26:28), We are told the blood covers our sins and washes us clean so we can approach God (Heb. 9:12–14).

Another way to look at animal sacrifice is that the killing of animals in Old Testament times was how people demonstrated their faith and trust in the supernatural. Today Christians do this by donating their time and treasure for the benefit of others. Although it is seen as a foolish act for those who do not believe, this significant sacrifice by followers appears to demonstrate faith and love for the Lord and each other.

Also, consider the strange practice of baptism to represent our belief in Jesus. It is meaningless in the eyes of the non-believer, yet profoundly significant in the lives of God's children and to God. Baptism is like the sacrifice of an animal in this way: somehow, submission to the significance of something that does not come naturally shows one's faith in, trust in, and love for the supernatural God.

Although the blood sacrifice of an animal was prescribed in the Bible for a covenant, to demonstrate our faith, and for the remission of sins (Heb. 9:22), was the sacrifice of Jesus the only permanent way to achieve these requirements and provide for our salvation? In trying to comprehend the cross fully, we may contemplate that the loving, sacrificial death of God's Son is the most seemingly senseless loving act ever conceived. It is incomprehensible that an eternal, all-powerful God loves us so deeply and intimately that He would become a man and voluntarily suffer and die to restore a relationship with us. It might be that only what seems the most foolish act of love ever conceived could communicate the undeserved and unearned love and forgiveness we needed for salvation (1 Cor. 1:18–31). The other option for Jesus would have been to take power and restore order, but how would we know such great love if there had not been a cross? How would we know the greatest act we can do is to sacrifice ourselves for others?

This brings up the question: How can the God of the New Testament—who loves us this much in the person of Jesus—be the same God in the Old Testament who demonstrates His wrath? The picture of a vengeful yet loving God who makes a law of death for eating a fruit is not a correct one (Gen. 2:17). A better way to look at it is that God is the source of life; without Him, we will die. Death is more of a truth about what happens without God's sustaining presence than a punishment.

The Bible is not a story of God's wrath but a love story of God seeking to save humanity from its self-imposed destruction and to restore the relationship humans were made to have with Him. In the Old Testament, to save humans from themselves, God allowed them to experience the consequences of their actions and continually led them back to Himself. What appears as God's wrath is Him turning humans over to the deserved consequences of their actions instead of continuing to pardon them. Even humans know that, on specific occasions, allowing people to suffer the consequences of their actions is the most loving thing to do. The story throughout the Bible is the true story of God's great love as He faithfully worked with rebellious humans.

To understand the story of God's great love, we need to re-visit the account of Adam and Eve. They had a healthy, free, and loving relationship with God. In the "cool of the day," God walked and talked with Adam and Eve in one of those just-right, loving friendships we crave (Gen. 3:8, NASB). In love, God gave Adam and Eve all things, except He instituted one boundary for their protection: "You must not eat from the tree of the knowledge of good and evil" (Gen. 2:17, NET). This presented an opportunity for a decision; Adam needed to either trust and rely on God to teach and provide for him, or he could seek the knowledge of right and wrong on his own. God knew Adam and Eve were far from ready to experience total autonomy, living apart from His direction. He knew it would destroy humanity if Adam chose against Him. People would not yet know how to handle themselves without His guidance. Unfettered knowledge of good and evil would lead to great wickedness and consistently selfish and often evil thoughts (Gen. 6:5). Knowing God's love, we are right to assume that God did not want Adam to make the wrong choice.

To prevent Adam and Eve from making this destructive choice, God used the idea of death as a communication tool to demonstrate the destruction they would bring to their lives personally and to future humanity with their sin. He did not say death was the punishment; instead, He warned they would die if they turned against Him (Gen. 2:16–17). When they disobeyed, they immediately felt guilt and shame. They began a life controlled by the knowledge of good and evil and instant separation from God. This was the outcome of their decision to learn on their own and go it alone without Him (Gen. 3:4–7).

Allowing them to live in their rebellion, God showed grace towards Adam and Eve by slaughtering a lamb to cover their guilt, the guilt that separated them from Him (Gen. 3:21). This was the beginning of the practice of blood sacrifice as a substitutionary death to atone for sin so humans could approach God. Even with the blood of an animal, the fact that they could no longer remain in the garden did not change (Gen. 3:22–24). Outside of paradise, they were given the curse of struggle in their attempt to provide for themselves and likely curtail their sin and pride (Gen. 3:16–19). Humans appear to need difficulties to teach us what is important. In times without struggle, we quickly forget to acknowledge God, and in success, we may also begin to imagine our greatness over others around us (Gen. 4:17–24). Eventually, God did allow Adam and Eve's death after an exceedingly long life. Death is not what God intended for humans and that is why death feels inherently wrong after our relatively short lives. We were meant to live forever in a garden, experiencing a relationship with God.

In the next chapter of Genesis, Adam's first son, Cain, murdered his younger brother Abel. With brother now killing brother, this was evidence that the broken relationship between God and humanity was severely affecting human relationships (Gen. 4:8; 1 John 3:11–12). The murder illustrated the consequences of the destroyed trust. Humans would now build their kingdoms by any means necessary. As the population grew and progressed, they continued to distrust God and take matters into their own hands which lead to more brokenness and pain in the world. A relationship cannot exist without trust, and humans were now born with an inherent bent to disbelieve God and His goodness. Fellowship with God became more and more distant because of rebellion and sin.

The flood now became the great fulfillment of God's prophecy of death. He brought death to all of mankind and all breathing creatures. Humans had decided to embrace their sin and do whatever was right in their own eyes. Some even think fallen angels physically joined in this revelry. Far from the intimate companionship of a person-to-person relationship we were meant for, it was a great corruption of God's intended purpose of creation, especially a perversion of His desire for humans. The abomination humanity had eroded to was incurable.

Fortunately, Noah pleased God, and He started over with Noah and his family. This time, God instituted a covenant with mankind, instructing us not to kill one another and not to kill animals except for food or as a recognition of God's mercy. Through a story about nakedness, the writer of Genesis also illustrated the sacredness of the marriage bond and the wickedness of sexual waywardness. From this point on, God promised not to destroy the earth again with a flood. He did not make this promise because He thought humans would now be righteous but because God had the plan of the cross to restore them to their true purpose despite their failures. He intended to redeem His children and show humans His love for them (Gen. 12:1–3)

The Bible then jumps forward to Abraham. God promised to use him to fulfill His plan of redemption by giving him numerous offspring, and the entire world would be blessed through one of his descendants (Gen. 12:1–3). It was a strange thing to promise to a ninety-year-old man who had no children. When Abraham finally had his miracle child, Isaac, the Lord asked Abraham to take the life of his chosen son. Abraham loved and trusted God so deeply that he faithfully took Isaac to Mount Moriah. He fully intended to sacrifice him there, believing God would raise him from the dead (Gen. 8:22–14; Heb. 11:17–19). An angel of the Lord stopped the sacrifice and provided a substitution. Abraham was blessed for his faith and willingness to be the one to restore humanity's relationship with God.

Despite Abraham's faith, Isaac's death would not have been sufficient to restore humanity's lost relationship with God because he was not a willing, nor a sinless, sacrifice. Sinlessness is a requirement because someone already deserving of punishment has no ability to pay another's penalty. Only the death of the sinless Son of the heavenly Father, God Himself, could mend the break of the relationship for humans to reach God. Only the death of a sinless, earthly Son could mend the relationship with God toward humans. God gave His heavenly Son, Jesus, to repair man's rebellion against Him, and humans unknowingly gave God their earthly Son, Jesus, to mend their guilt and shame. This reconciliation could only have been accomplished in one man, Jesus Christ, the sinless sacrifice. He was both the "Son of Man" who paid the price for humanity's sin and the "Son of God" who gave Himself up to restore a loving relationship between God and man (Matt. 18:11; John 1:49).

The Father did not kill Jesus, and humanity did not kill Jesus (John 10:17–18). It may seem that the Father forced Jesus to die, but Jesus was a willing participant at every moment of His death. Motivated by His great love for us and His desire to have a relationship with us, He chose His death, a horrific death, to once and for all demonstrate the grace and forgiveness needed to restore the loving relationship lost in the garden.

We can hardly imagine the immense love Jesus demonstrated as He submitted Himself to the whipping and the brutal death on the cross. At each blow, His love endured as He restrained His power to obliterate the perpetrator. The ancient Jewish prophet Isaiah wrote: "By His stripes we are healed" (Isaiah 53:5, NKJV). His gruesome torture and death were for an important reason. He took on the violence we deserve for our sins. In His love, Jesus paid the penalty and endured the destruction our sin caused so we could be healed, freed from our enslavement to destruction, and invited to enter a relationship with Him.

His death was the perfect payment to appease justice, provide mercy, and pave the way for a mutually loving relationship extending from God toward people and from people toward God. The cross ended the need for the law and punishment. Jesus' sacrificial death demonstrated transformation through love, opening the way to the *good life* the Father intended, free from the judgment and violence of the law.

When Jesus came to restore eternal life and repair humanity's relationship with Him, no conditions were put on our behavior before He would exercise His love for us. Jesus told Nicodemus, long before He was crucified, "For God so loved the world that He gave His only begotten Son, that whoever believes in Him should not perish but have everlasting life" (John 3:16, NKJV). All anyone must do to receive restoration of God's love is to believe in and accept Jesus as Lord (Rom. 10:9–10). His love does not come with any stipulations to fulfill or hoops to jump through prior to Him loving us. Jesus died for us "while we were still sinners" (Rom. 5:8, NET).

In His great love, God forgave the sins of the whole world through Jesus on the cross. The apostle John also wrote: "He Himself is the propitiation for our sins, and not for ours only, but also for those of the whole world" (1 John 2:2, HCSB). Jesus was so completely driven by His love for us that He took upon Himself all the sins of each and every human. John the Baptist exclaimed upon seeing Jesus: "Here is the Lamb of God, who takes away the sin of the world" (John 1:29, HCSB). The cross was an act of sacrificial love that provided forgiveness and atonement for all human sins—to restore the possibility of a relationship with God for every human (Rom. 5:18). Our reconciliation was predicated on His love for all humanity--shown on the cross (John 3:16).

Paul goes to great ends to communicate how immense and permanent the love of God is for us when we choose to follow Him:

> What then are we to say about these things? If God is for us, who is against us? He did not even spare His own Son but offered Him up for us all; how will He not also with Him grant us everything? ...Who can separate us from the love of Christ? Can affliction or anguish or persecution or famine or nakedness or danger or sword? ...No, in all these things we are more than victorious through Him who loved us. For I am persuaded that not even death or life, angels or rulers, things present or things to come, hostile powers, height or depth, or any other created thing will have the power to separate us from the love of God that is in Christ Jesus our Lord!
>
> Romans 8:31–32, 35, 37–39 (HCSB)

The story of God's great love and sacrifice on the cross, so we might know His love and be restored to a relationship with Him, is the amazingly good news that all believers should proclaim. It should be spoken of to those who do not know God's real love, and it needs to be declared as the desperately needed answer to what has killed our souls and destined us to hell.

Our trust in the loving, brutal act of the cross as the means of forgiveness for our sins is the seemingly foolish act of faith we must commit to change our hearts from the inside out. Jesus' humble sacrifice freed us from a life of sin and death. When He died for our sins, He made it possible for the Spirit to live inside us, guiding us in His love. We can be forever transformed and deeply moved by knowing of and believing in this strange act of sacrifice. On the cross, Jesus showed a new way of love that was intensely superior to any achievement that the world would have deemed worthy of a savior. He demonstrated that His love was even more important than His own life. If a person can comprehend such an amazing act of love, how could they not respond positively to this love, a love with the ability to turn our lives *love-side-up*?

., and when His sacrifice is emulated, the cross transforms human interactions. It was an act of love so great it completely redefined what love is and how we are to show love for one another.

Chapter 12: Worthy to Travel

He made Him who knew no sin to be sin on our behalf, so that we might become the righteousness of God in Him.

Second Corinthians 5:21 (NASB)

AS A YOUNG CHRISTIAN seeking to be good, I thought I could only know whether I was good and worthy to be in God's presence if I lived according to the rules in the Bible. I attempted to achieve righteousness by becoming a good person who broke no laws and did good instead of evil. I told you about the extensive list of sins I made as a high school senior and how I struggled with following it. It may not be easy to understand, but that way of thinking is the product of religious works and is part of our fleshly effort to make ourselves righteous. When I lived under the law to be righteous, at times, I was a law abider, and at other times a lawbreaker. I was either a slave to the law to become morally righteous or a slave in my rebellion against the moral law.

For most of my life, I considered righteousness to be a state of doing what is right in a moral sense. G. W. Bromiley's Bible dictionary explains righteousness as a state of a covenant relationship, not as an accomplishment of ethical behavior:

> In the OT, righteousness involves the fulfillment of the demands of a relationship …the OT usually has the covenant with Yahweh in view (e.g., Isa. 51:7; Ezk. 18:19, 21) …When a person fulfills the obligations of a relationship, that person is said to be righteous. [15]

At the time of Christ, before the cross, righteousness had changed to a measurable degree: The qualities associated with righteousness include mercy, generosity, honesty, moderation, and active concern for the poor and oppressed; qualities of unrighteousness include greed, violence, and oppression ...Righteous persons generally are those whose merits outweigh their transgressions.[16]

The Pharisees understood righteousness as doing what is right according to the law, where the good are "rewarded and the wicked punished."[17] What Christ demonstrated on the cross clarified the definition of righteousness:

In the NT, one finds again the primacy of the relational aspect of righteousness. The righteous are those who participate in and preserve a covenant relationship with God or other persons. God's righteousness is shown in that He has saved humanity in Christ. [18]

Paul further developed the meaning of righteousness. In his writings Bromley concluded:

Only the righteousness of God revealed in the cross and granted to the believer through faith in Christ can defeat death and reconcile a person to God. ...Thus, the righteousness of God cannot be a mere property, ethical attribute, or quality. The righteousness of God in the cross is the saving link between God and sinful humanity; no ethical attribute can ever endure the stress of being such a connection.[19]

It is unclear if righteousness was ever intended to be achieved by following the law. The apostle Paul indicated that Abraham's righteousness was not through the law but through his faith in God. He also surmised that King David's idea of righteousness came from forgiveness, not works. Paul wrote:

> For if Abraham was declared righteous by the works of the law, he has something to boast about—but not before God. For what does the Scripture say? "Abraham believed God, and it was credited to him as righteousness." Now to the one who works, his pay is not credited due to grace but due to obligation. But to the one who does not work but believes in the one who declares the ungodly righteous, his faith is credited as righteousness. So even David himself speaks regarding the blessedness of the man to whom God credits righteousness apart from works: "Blessed are those whose lawless deeds are forgiven, and whose sins are covered; blessed is the one against whom the Lord will never count sin."
>
> Romans 4:2–8 (NET)

Abraham and David each committed grave sinful actions during their lives. We could include other prominent Old Testament figures in the list of the unrighteous because of their deeds—including Isaac, Jacob, and all of Jacob's sons. The members of this "cloud of witnesses" all pleased God by their faith in Him and not by their ability to follow the law with their works (Heb. 12:1, NET). They were destined to receive the righteousness of God and a perfect relationship with Him—and they did, "together with us" (Heb. 11:40, NET).

The Israelites attempted to obey the law, but this did not make them worthy to be in God's presence. Paul explained, in his letter to the Romans, why the Israelites' understanding of establishing their righteousness was misled:

> For I can testify that they are zealous for God, but their zeal is not in line with the truth. For ignoring the righteousness that comes from God, and seeking instead to establish their own righteousness, they did not submit to God's righteousness. For Christ is the end of the law, with the result that there is righteousness for everyone who believes. For Moses writes about the righteousness that is by the law: "The one who does these

things will live by them." But the righteousness that is by faith says: "Do not say in your heart, 'Who will ascend into heaven?'" (that is, to bring Christ down) or "Who will descend into the abyss?" (that is, to bring Christ up from the dead). But what does it say? "The word is near you, in your mouth and in your heart" (that is, the word of faith that we preach).

Romans 10:2–8 (NET)

The first-century Jew's idea of self-made righteousness from following the Mosaic law was "not in line with the truth" (Rom. 10:2, NET). They sought to make themselves worthy of being in the presence of God. It appears God always intended to accept people into His presence by their faith alone, and it was a man-inspired movement to be righteous by obligation to the law. "Christ is the end of [using] the law [with the result that there is] ...righteousness to everyone who believes" (Rom. 10:4, NET). He is the end of using the law for the Jews to have a relationship with God, and from this also flows that the cross and the new covenant do not instruct Christians to use the Mosaic law for their sanctification either. Following the law does not bring Christ closer to us, and our sin against the law does not make Christ more significant. Our faith brings Christ into our mouths and hearts.

Righteousness for the Gentile believer also does not come through following the Mosaic Law or any other rules we can garner from the New Testament. Paul wrote that our righteousness is accomplished by the grace of God, through our faith in Jesus and His work on the cross:

> ... yet we know that no one is justified by the works of the law but by the faithfulness of Jesus Christ. And we have come to believe in Christ Jesus, so that we may be justified by the faithfulness of Christ and not by the works of the law, because by the works of the law no one will be justified. ... I do not set aside God's grace, because if righteousness could come through the law, then Christ died for nothing!"

Galatians 2:16, 21 (NET)

The burden of having to follow the law to be in covenant with God ended when Jesus completed the Mosaic covenant through His sinless life and the shedding of His blood. We can now receive righteousness as a gift, not something bound by our obedience to the Mosaic law. If we could be made righteous by following the law, it would dilute the need and purpose of the death of Jesus (Heb. 10:26–31). We have been made righteous by our faith in the Son of God and his work on the cross —apart from the law—or "Christ died for nothing." But we know that His death was not in vain.

Therefore, the righteousness of God is not achieved by a personal effort to sanctify ourselves. Our righteousness is solely found in the righteous act of Jesus on the cross, given to us because of our faith in Him. By faith, we receive forgiveness and the removal of sin, and we can renew our relationship with God—a relationship He intended from the beginning. A follower of Jesus is declared righteous, or sinless, the instant they put their faith in Him (2 Cor. 5:21).

Our faith is in the fact that Jesus paid the price of death for our sins at the cross, which not only removed the penalty of sin but also took away our sins, past, present, and future. It is not sufficient to say we are made righteous because we will no longer receive punishment for our actions; our sins must be taken away. When our sins are removed, and we are made righteous, our nature is changed from sinner to sinless, enabling us to enter an intimate relationship with God. This is the interaction with God that was intended for humans from the beginning of creation.

We are now justified to enter His presence. It may seem undeserved, but He has declared us righteous and our presence before God is now justified. The word "justified" might conjure images of someone making an excuse or a defense for their actions but it's a different type of justification. Our behavior as sinners is unjustifiable, and according to the old covenant, we are guilty of committing transgressions deserving punishment, including death, and we are forbidden from the presence of God. In the new covenant, we can stand before God as forgiven and miraculously regarded as a different person because we are righteous in Christ and not in danger of being cast out. To cast us out would be to cast Jesus out because He is in us and vouches for us.

God wants us to correctly understand that our source of righteousness is not attained by living according to the law. It is achieved by having faith in what Christ accomplished on the cross and sealed by the Holy Spirit in us. Any effort away from righteousness by faith and toward works according to law only produces personal righteousness of our own, which will not justify us (Rom. 10:3–4). The only source of God's righteousness is faith in God and reliance on the gift given at the cross.

Chapter 13: A New Way

How much more will the blood of Christ, who through the eternal Spirit offered himself without blemish to God, purify our consciences from dead works to worship the living God. And so he is the mediator of a new covenant, so that those who are called may receive the eternal inheritance he has promised, since he died to set them free from the violations committed under the first covenant.

Hebrews 9:14-15 (NET)

JESUS RANSOMED US FROM the inevitable destruction we deserved under the old covenant by His shed blood. By this same blood, He ended the old covenant and established a new covenant that frees us from the law and its consequences.

The new covenant is a new agreement between God and humanity to completely transform how we are sanctified. It removes the law as the means of sanctification and replaces it with the Spirit living in us. This changes the process of sanctification entirely, from a life of religion focused on removing our sin through confession, repentance, and works of righteousness defined by the law to a moment-by-moment adventure with the Spirit.

The terms of this new covenant are given by Jesus to His disciples just before the cross:

> A new commandment [Covenant] I give to you, that you love one another, even as I have loved you, that you also love one another. By this all men will know that you are My disciples, if you have love for one another.
>
> John 13:34–35 (NASB)

Therefore, the essence of our sanctification in the new covenant occurs when we seek the Spirit to help us live according to Jesus' one commandment to "love one another." The fundamental definition of sin for a believer was transformed from being understood as breaking the law to being redefined as a failure to love (Gal. 5:14).

Viewing sanctification as the Spirit enabling us to have an ever-increasing Christ-like love, rather than thinking the Spirit helps us to follow the law, is a foundational difference in understanding sanctification in the new covenant. Upon our belief, we now enter into a loving relationship with God, where love for our neighbors and ourselves flows out of that relationship.

Many find it difficult to accept that our ability to love as Jesus loves is the measure of our sanctification. They cannot let go of the idea that Christians are bettered by behavioral improvement according to external standards. Unfortunately, this old understanding of sanctification misses the foundational work of Christ. He wants to transform us into the image of God by growing us to love as He loved (2 Cor. 3:18). This is quite different from improvement according to the law.

Further confusion comes from what a believer sees as the purpose of grace. Is God's grace shown when He frees us from the law, forgives us, and takes away our sins, or does His grace free us from our deserved punishment for breaking the law and give us strength to follow the law in the future?

Individuals who believe we are sanctified by following the law and that grace is to help us accomplish that task will run into a few hard questions to answer. If we are not saved by works according to the Mosaic law, how can works sanctify us according to that same law or any new law? Attempting to determine precisely which laws to abide by seems entirely arbitrary. After we are justified and declared righteous by faith, must we still do additional works to be more right with God? Struggling to be sanctified according to the law is an impossible task that even grace cannot accomplish in a person.

Paul juxtaposes these two positions of sanctification clearly to the Galatians:

> You who are trying to be declared righteous by the law have been alienated from Christ; you have fallen away from grace! For through the Spirit, by faith, we wait expectantly for the hope

of righteousness. For in Christ Jesus neither circumcision nor uncircumcision carries any weight – the only thing that matters is faith working through love.

Galatians 5:4–6 (NET)

Sometimes, it is hard to see that "the only thing that matters is [our] faith working through love," especially when rulers, leaders, and pastors promote obedience to the law as the measuring point of our progress. Paul implies that obedience to the law is not even close to what sanctification is for the believer. Jesus created a way to have a relationship with us that did not involve enslavement to rules and constant condemnation. He took on our deserved violence for us, so we no longer need to live under the threat of the violence of the law for our sanctification.

Living by the law is an attempt to overcome sin via the flesh. We try to use our strength and ability to follow the law to overcome our needs and desires that predestine our sins. The new law of the life-giving Spirit is quite different (Rom. 8:2). God's Spirit in us overcomes the flesh. The Spirit fills us with His love, and that love moves us to love like Jesus. When filled with His love, we can achieve selfless love for God and our neighbor. This selfless, unconditional love fulfills the whole law. The law cannot make us more loving and thus more sanctified; that is not what the law does. Under the new covenant, the only resemblance of law for the believer is the commandment to love as Jesus loved. Following the Mosaic law to be sanctified is not a part of the new covenant.

When we follow Jesus, we don't merely exchange the law of Moses for a better law found in the New Testament (Gal. 2:21). Jesus fulfilled and ended the covenant of the law once and for all, and the new covenant, or system of freedom from the law, is given to those who believe.

This is especially important to understand when we explain the blessings of Jesus to a Muslim or a Mormon, for they are following predominantly works-based religions. We should not attempt to convince them that our religion has a better law; instead, we should try to show them that sin and the law eventually destroy us. We should point them to Jesus, who takes away sin and the law and gives us His Spirit to live and love by.

Those who still live under the law for their sanctification do not understand the new covenant we are in and are blocked from seeing the freedom and truth we have in Jesus: "But until this very day whenever Moses is read, a veil lies over their minds" (2 Cor. 3:15, NET). When we begin to understand the end of the law, it is like a veil is removed. The fading glory that comes and goes with the ability to follow the law disappears. "And we all, with unveiled faces reflecting the glory of the Lord, are being transformed into the same image from one degree of glory to another, which is from the Lord, who is the Spirit" (2 Cor. 3:18, NET). We are given new glory, and this glory is amazing because it gives us the gift of continually walking in God's presence, never separated from Him by any action or thought.

To put it another way, the goal of sanctification under the new covenant is to become a more loving person by demonstrating the love of the cross in our lives. Religion's concept of good and Jesus' concept of good diverge at this point. In religion, goodness comes by following a list of rules, leading to a practical level of sanctification if you succeed and condemnation if you fail. New covenant goodness comes through embracing Jesus' sacrifice on the cross to make us good. We are good only through faith in God, by which we are declared good. Then, in response to God's gift of goodness and unconditional forgiveness and love, we love with God's love in the power of the Spirit.

The believer's sanctification materializes as the Spirit teaches us to love with the sacrificial love of the cross. This is evidenced when we become loving in our hearts and demonstrate His love through our words and deeds. Change happens as Christians become, on the outside (in their flesh), the person God has already transformed them into on the inside—in their spirit (Gal. 2:20).

Jesus established a new covenant in which He takes sin away by removing the law, reconciling our relationship with God, and giving us newfound freedom and power to make loving decisions. Freed from all condemnation and lavished with love, our sanctification comes from an entirely different mindset. It comes from a new life in Christ as we walk with the Spirit and learn to love God, our neighbors, and ourselves. Our life's goal should not be to collect blessings by following the right rules to keep us from sinning;

instead, we are to discover how much love we can give when we live by the Spirit in our relationship with God.

We follow a Savior who gave up His life for us to demonstrate His love. Jesus is growing this love in us as we become more and more like Him, living a life worthy of His presence in us and worthy of the new life He has given us. His ultimate goal is to move us from a state of slavery to sin, where we are separated from Him under the law—whether the core cause is living against the law or living by the law—and to bring us into a state of relationship with Him, freely perfected in His love through the power and guidance of the Holy Spirit. This is truly the process of sanctification under the new covenant established by the cross.

Chapter 14: Why Not Take the Old Way?

For Christ is the end of the law.

Romans 10:4 (NET)

AFTER HAVING MANY CONVERSATIONS with believers on the role of the law in a Christian's life, I know I must explain further about our freedom from sin and especially freedom from the law. It is shocking for most to consider that Christ was the end of the law.

I was in a small youth group meeting one night and a leader spoke up and confessed he had broken all the Ten Commandments. He said this to make the point that Christians do not follow the law. The room went silent, and I was in a state of shock, intentionally holding back my reaction to the awkwardness of the situation. It appeared we were in a room full of believers who trusted the law to make people good, or at least not kill one another. This leader had just openly admitted that not even the Ten Commandments was working for him, and he had broken them all.

Finally, a young woman cautiously said, "I guess I am okay with you breaking nine of the commandments, but the 'Thou shall not murder' one makes me a little uncomfortable."

The leader explained that he had once given a young lady a ride to an abortion clinic. His explanation seemed to ease the tension concerning violence but didn't remove our discomfort with his confession of the other nine. Removing and replacing the law with people doing what is right in their own eyes is clearly perceived as detrimental. The youth leader's suggestion of the law's irrelevance brought fear because he did not explain how it was replaced with the new life of love found in Christ Jesus.

Humans continually find themselves circling back to the same question: What is the best way to fix humanity? Is it enforcing laws like the Ten Commandments? More narrowly focused, is following the Mosaic law the right way to fix the Christian? Should Christians follow the law at all?

My experience tells me that the Messianic Jews and many other sects of Christianity would give a resounding "yes" to both questions. At the same time, recent quasi-antinomians—like Andy Stanley, Andrew Farley, and Aaron Budjen—are opposed to the idea of using the law to achieve a form of righteousness and to bring about the believer's sanctification.

Andy Stanley, a writer, pastor, and founder of the enormously impacting North Point Ministries, states in his book *Irresistible*: "Participants in the new covenant are not required to obey most of the commandments found in the first half of their Bibles."[20]

Andrew Farley is the pastor of Church Without Religion and the author of *God Without Religion*. In his book, he clearly explains and defends the end of the Mosaic covenant, and our new directive is to not mix law with the grace found in the new covenant.[21]

Aaron Budjen, a former rabbi turned Christian pastor and host of the Living God Ministries radio program, vehemently opposes using the law to establish righteousness. He believes obeying the law to be righteous nullifies the death of Christ.[22]

These three men, and many others, have used an avalanche of scriptures, combined with a clear understanding of the gospel, to show that we are not to use the Mosaic law to attain personal sanctification.

Antinomian may not be the most popular term preferred by the new grace movement in America, but it appears to be fitting. Antinomianism "is the belief that the Christian is no longer under the law."[23] This term was coined by Martin Luther when describing the ideas of his friend, Johannes Agricola. These men grew up together as friends in the city of Eisleben, Germany. They later worked intimately together at the beginning of the Reformation. The divide began when Agricola objected to Luther's use of the law. Agricola became uncomfortable with the dissonance between justification by grace through faith, which frees the believer from the law, and the Lutheran preachers of his day using the law for a guide to the Christian life and discipline. He then began to develop doctrines challenging whether the law should be brought up at all in the Christian life. When Luther sent out secular authorities to judge pastors as to whether their lives lived up to the Biblical law, he became very upset. Agricola wrote that the moral law, itself, was "for the courthouse and not for Christians." He believed the Christian life was to be lived by grace alone and not to be judged by law, especially not in the hands of secular authorities. Luther differed from Agricola in that Luther believed in using the condemnation of the law to convict the Christians of their sin, demonstrating their need for the gospel of grace. In the midst of this controversy, Luther wrote his objections to Agricola's idea of grace alone in his essays entitled, "Against the Antinomians," forever coining the word to describe those who don't think Christians should live according to the law.[24]

How can I and others be against using the law in the Christian's life to please God when so much of Christianity embraces its use? To encourage obedience to the law, pastors often use these verses from the first chapter of Joshua.

> Carefully obey all the law my servant Moses charged you to keep! Do not swerve from it to the right or to the left, so that you may be successful in all you do. This law scroll must not leave your lips! You must memorize it day and night so you can carefully obey all that is written in it. Then you will prosper and be successful.
>
> Joshua 1:7–8 (NET)

The promise of earthly blessings is an enticing temptation but using it for moral motivation ignores that rarely did anyone achieve sustained good behavior. Joshua implied that those who obey the law would receive blessings. But blessings only came to those who could abide by the law. No one to my knowledge, except Jesus, has claimed that they obeyed it completely. Using the threats and rewards of the law has never worked on the fallen, so why keep using it?

The law is impossible for the common person to follow, but an even worse situation existed for the priest. The physically defective priest could only partially obey the priestly duties. God told Moses to write this instruction:

> Say to Aaron: 'For the generations to come none of your descendants who has a defect may come near to offer the food of his God. ...no man who is blind or lame, disfigured or deformed; no man with a crippled foot or hand, or who is a hunchback or a dwarf, or who has any eye defect, or who has festering or running sores. ...No descendant of Aaron the priest who has any defect is to come near to present the food offerings to the Lord. ...he must not go near the curtain or approach the altar, and so desecrate my sanctuary.'
>
> Leviticus 21:17–21, 23 (NIV)

Only pure, unblemished priests could approach God's presence. A blemished descendant of Aaron could never achieve complete righteousness. In this decree, the law foreshadows that all humans are powerless to achieve righteousness through the law because we are all blemished. We need grace because we are not capable of following the law.

We might still want to cling to the law and Joshua's promise, but maybe not all of it. Generally, believers would like to see the Ten Commandments promoted and upheld. While this can be good for the benefit of a society, the old covenant laws—even the ones written on stone—are no longer a source for contention between God and us. Consider what Paul wrote: "...for the letter kills, but the Spirit gives life ...the ministry that produced death—carved in letters on stone tablets— ...produced condemnation" (2 Cor. 3:6–7, 9, NET). Not even the Ten Commandments were spared from Paul's argument for the removal of the law from the believer.

A universal law like the Ten Commandments may seem to bring a sense of safety and comfort but this is not usually the result. We often think that if we hang the commandments in a courthouse or codify the law with ecclesiastical or governmental power, we will have established a solution to our problems. At best, we have forced compliance to a solution but not fixed the problem. The problem usually lies much deeper than a law could ever fix.

The law is not wrong in deterring evil with the threat of punishment or even death, but it can only provide a temporary hiatus from a condition that will not be fixed by behavior correction. For a time, people—individually and as a society—may experience transformation through ethical ideas and moral directions. Yet, a law-based system's effectiveness is usually short-lived because humans are in a state of decay. Read the biblical books from Judges through Chronicles for an example, or merely observe today's moral climate.

Some may see good things happening in the general morality of society today. They may like the new ethic of kindness and tolerance. Modern governments appear to show more grace by shedding their attachment to deterrent punishment for moral transgression and by giving expanded moral freedom by redefining what a transgression is. No matter how far society goes in this experiment, to control disapproved behavior, they will eventually need to set boundaries or unredeemed people will take advantage of one another.

A functioning society must have a system of control, even if it decides to change morality and drastically change the values of its subjects. Without proactively instituting morals to replace the previous abandoned system, people will again become uncontrollably evil as they were in the days of Noah. And, as in all utopias that humans have attempted so far, those who refuse to agree with the new system must be silenced or eliminated for the good of the system.

Paul, too, like many contemporary utopian thinkers, promoted freedom from the law and the shedding of punishment, but only because he knew the love of the cross, the blessings of the new life in Christ, and the power of the Spirit in him. To try to achieve a utopia that mimics the grace and freedom of Christ—without the Spirit to guide us in the way of the cross—is a recipe for disaster.

In Romans chapters 6–8, Paul argues that the law will not bring sanctification, only condemnation. Concluding that the law was completed, Paul wrote, "the law of the life-giving Spirit in Christ Jesus has set you free from the law of sin and death" (Rom. 8:2, NET). The law brought precisely that— "sin and death." The Mosaic law seemed only to make people more aware of their sins and to show them the impossibility of achieving perfection through their efforts (Rom. 7). It demonstrates that a person cannot be righteous and loving through striving. And even if someone got close to following the law, did they perform their deeds in love?

When Paul refers to the law as the "law of sin and death," he clearly describes its outcome (Rom. 8:2, NET). Under the law, death was instituted by God as a deterrent to restrain humans from rebellion and sin. Death for behavior did not start with the law. Death began its reign with Adam and Eve in the garden when they rebelled. Humanity became so irredeemable at the time of Noah that God's only choice was to wipe them out in a great and sweeping death. With the addition of the Mosaic law, many transgressions were prescribed the death penalty; it was literally the "ministry that produced death" (Second Corinthians 3:7, NET).

The law is insufficient to make us righteous and is powerless to bring people into a loving relationship with God, ourselves, and our neighbors. However, the law's capacity to convict is exponentially more powerful than our aptitude to overcome sin. The law will condemn us until we are lowered to the status of a worm. In the face of its conviction, if we can stand at all, we will stand condemned. How can one use this instrument of condemnation to attain sanctification and live the new life that Jesus gives?

Paul wrote directly about the end of the law in his letter to the church in Colossae:

> Having wiped out the handwriting of requirements that was against us, which was contrary to us. And He has taken it out of the way, having nailed it to the cross. Having disarmed principalities and powers, He made a public spectacle of them, triumphing over them in it.
>
> Colossians 2:14–15 (NKJV)

Jesus' plan was to wipe out the written requirements by which we judge. In doing this, He not only removed the law but also took away the power of those in charge of enforcing the law. If we then entrust new "principalities and powers" to give us a Christian list of sins, we are starting the sin condemnation cycle all over again, working to recreate a substitution of the law that Jesus nailed to the cross.

It is misguided to think we can somehow discover a better law to facilitate our works of righteousness now that we have grace. We should be living free from the law of sin and death, old or new, and instead be living by the Spirit and in the grace He provided. God's goal for humans, even when we were under the law, has always been for us to love Him, our neighbors, and ourselves. The law of Moses, given to help achieve that goal, could not bring it to completion and often brings the opposite result (Rom. 8:3).

In our new life with Jesus, sins according to an old covenant law should no longer be the issue. This idea is illustrated in the lives of the gentile believers. Acts 15 presents the record of a historic meeting of church leaders in Jerusalem. These men discussed whether Gentiles were obligated to follow the law as believers in Jesus. They decided Gentiles should instead follow some general moral obligations unrelated to the law of Moses. The case should have been closed after this council, but it was not. In Galatia, Paul ran into men who wanted Gentile converts to be circumcised. Paul argued that following the law to become right would alienate the Gentiles from Christ. Instead of following the law, he said, "The only thing that matters is faith working through love" (Gal. 5:6, NET).

While the law brought temporary glory for those willing and able to live by it, it quickly faded into condemnation when they failed to follow it consistently. At some point, everyone fails, their glory fades, and they are condemned.

> For if there was glory in the ministry that produced condemnation, how much more does the ministry that produces righteousness excel in glory! For indeed, what had been glorious now has no glory because of the tremendously greater glory of what replaced it.
>
> Second Corinthians 3:9–10 (NET)

Through Christ's death, every believer can enter and stay in God's glory (2 Cor. 5:14). This permanent glory comes through Jesus, not the fading glory of following the law.

What then should the believer do with the Mosaic law in the process of sanctification, since it is not used as a source of guilt and condemnation? The law is crucial for knowing God and learning His wisdom concerning life. In it, we can find tremendous knowledge about human behavior, and we can learn boundaries concerning how to love God, our neighbor, and ourselves in a community structure. Unfortunately, believers have regularly employed it to create an exceedingly long list of do's and don'ts. Even though no one can come close to abiding by the list, it is an effective system by which we can clobber and destroy our neighbors and ourselves (Matt. 23:13–39). That was not God's intention. He wanted humans to love His law and see its true purpose and goal. Instead, the law seemed to bring pride and control for the ones who kept it and complete wretchedness for the ones who turned from it.

It is good news that we no longer need to live under the law to become morally righteous. If the law could not make the Israelites behave, it certainly would not succeed with the Gentiles. Fortunately, our worthiness to stand before God will not be based on our works according to the law since Christ has already given us His righteousness.

Ultimately, before Christ, the only way for humans to complete the covenant of the law was through their earthly death and a future of deserved punishment. On the cross, Christ fulfilled the requirement of death, enabling a way to end the reign of death in our lives and begin a new reign of life. The old covenant, found in the Mosaic law, was a part of that reign of death, and that reign was completed and ended with Jesus dying on the cross. The crucifixion of Jesus was not just the end of the old covenant, but it also established a new one; which I am looking forward to discussing after we finish with sin.

Chapter 15: Breaking Down

The sting of death is sin, and the power of sin is the law.

First Corinthians 15:56 (NET)

I WAS THE VICTIM OF violence for the first nineteen years of my life. As a young child of six, I sat alone, crying, huddled in a corner while my father violently beat my mother. From that point on, I transformed from a happy kid to a somewhat depressed child. I entered a life of survival and envisioned that someday I would escape.

When my father disapproved of my mother's actions and wanted to change her behavior, he used violence. My father's heinous physical abuse and destructive words were unacceptable, hurtful, and extremely damaging. While horrendous violence is atypical of humans, we are all capable of performing awful actions and saying hurtful things to force others to change and comply with our wishes—attempting to meet our needs and wants.

Most of us show restraint and self-control in public, but in private, we may self-righteously turn on the ones we love most. Receiving Jesus and acknowledging His sacrifice on the cross should free us from a life of violence, and it can, but we must be willing to accept His help. If we're not willing to humbly allow His healing transformation, the brokenness in our brain and flesh will not be fixed. This seemed to be the case for my father and too many other Christians.

Warning! The following story may contain triggers for some readers.

During my first year in college, I journaled about one of my parent's fights when I was a teenager. I recalled it well because it was such a traumatic experience.

My mom moved about once a year when I was a child. We fled to a safer life but stayed in a one-hundred-and-fifty-mile radius, covering parts of Northern Wyoming and Southern Montana. Although it seemed far as a child, it never was far enough to get away from the dysfunction of my father.

My mom, Margaret, finished hooking the utilities to yet another trailer house. She had unusual talents for a woman in those days. The trailer was parked in one of the trashiest trailer courts in Billings, Montana—a dump with gravel roads and no fences and not far from the sugar beet factory. We could smell the stink of boiling beets all winter, which smelled a bit like a sour kitchen sink. My mother had moved this trailer 120 miles from Cody, Wyoming—where we'd previously lived.

She called it the "Corinthian Trailer," which sounded grand but was merely the manufacturer's name. She had purchased the Corinthian in a salvage auction for five hundred dollars. It had experienced a minor fire, damaging the rear of the trailer. There was an attempt to fix it, but it was never finished, so we lived with a mix of rough wood floors, unpainted drywall, and charred paneling. The odor of burned toxic materials competed with the smell of the beet factory. On top of the strained living conditions, she would fill the trailer from floor to ceiling with boxes and other wall-to-wall clutter to comfort her need to own things.

She owned a lot of stuff, including several other trailers and houses, most of which we lived in at different times. If I had to pick my favorite trailer to live in, it was the "Red and White Trailer," named for obvious reasons. The others were the "Yellow Trailer," the "Star Trailer," and two houses with nicknames, the "Green House" and the "Klucas House." These were the valued possessions she had accumulated over the years from working as a teacher, cook, waitress, laundry worker, landlord, and other odd jobs. She liked owning property—a symbol of escape and shelter from poverty and violence.

Most of our homes were halfway remodeled and all were piled full of boxes of clothes my mother had found in the garbage at a secondhand store called "The Bargain Box." Her messy houses were burdensome on my childhood because I could never invite friends over.

While living in the Corinthian trailer in Billings, Mom moved the Red and White Trailer into a space near us when I was fourteen. I hoped my dream—of a home, a place clean and free from the clutter of boxes and junk—might be fulfilled if I could move into this trailer. I wanted a place to bring a friend over and not be ashamed.

She agreed to let me move in, which allowed me to spend two weeks in a nice home. I could walk all over the house without navigating a maze of boxes or stepping over trash on the floor. I especially liked that I was not living in the middle of a remodel project.

One weekend, my father, Wayne, drove the 135-mile trek from the small town of Greybull, Wyoming, population 1500. (I had many bad memories of Greybull because of the cruelty of the kids I grew up with. When Mom and Dad divorced the year before, I chose to live with her in Billings to escape that town.) By now, Mom had a boyfriend, but even with another man in the picture, Dad still tried to get back together with Mom. (They eventually remarried when I was in tenth grade, but they rarely lived together until Mom could no longer live on her own.)

When he heard Mom was moving the Red and White Trailer to Billings, he expected her to rent it since it would cost money to have it there. I think he was paying some of the expenses for the move and wanted it to be a source of income for her. After finding out I'd moved in, he informed me that my mother had agreed to rent it and that I needed to move back to the burned, box-cluttered trailer. (Later, Mom denied agreeing to it, but things were confusing with her; she would say what she needed to say to make people happy or to get out of trouble.)

I wanted to cry from the sadness and disappointment I felt. I somehow knew my new living arrangements were too good to be true. Mom offered me the bigger back bedroom in the Corinthian, which was a loving attempt to make living in a mess a little easier but it did not help the sadness.

My father had planned to leave early, since they were not married, but that evening he refused to leave. Finally, he and my mother started arguing, probably about her boyfriend, Tom. She was still sleeping with Tom on occasion, and he was probably hiding in a nearby trailer to avoid my father. Either way, I am sure the fight began when my mother rejected my dad's sexual advances. He began making profanity-laden accusations about Mom visiting Tom because she kept going to the neighbor's house during the day. He guessed that Tom was there and violently accused Mom of having sex with him, which Mom insisted was not true.

Dad slung horrible names, allegations of adultery, and profanity-laced accusations. She denied everything and twisted her answers to attempt to calm down the situation, but there was no end to his temper.

He grabbed her hair and jerked her around as he yelled about how he would extract his retribution for her adultery.

"Stop, Wayne. You're hurting me. Please stop," she wailed.

I lay in my bed, gritting my teeth. He was hurting my mother. My father had done this countless times. I was not a little kid anymore who hid in some corner, alone and powerless to do anything.

Earlier that day I had told myself I would prevent them from physically fighting. If I didn't intervene, it would tear me apart. I thought about the club I had made that was hidden in the bottom of my closet. Finally, although frightened of the unknown, I jumped out of bed, grabbed my club, ran down the hall, and yelled, "Let go of her, or I'll kill you!"

My father, astonished, let go of my mother and they both stared at me. At sixty-four, he was much stronger than I was, but with the club, I was more of a threat to him.

"I could have you put in jail for this." He glared at me.

"Go ahead, but you're not going to touch her." Fear started to grip me. "Get out of here, just get out of here," I yelled.

He stood his ground as I waited for him to jump me.

My mother stepped in. "Wayne, you better leave."

He left the trailer and got into his van.

"Ernie, put down the club," she said.

Tears rolled down my cheeks. "No, Mother, he is not going to hurt you anymore. I won't let him."

"Okay, calm down. I'm going to talk to him."

"Why?" I felt like she was undermining what I had accomplished.

She returned half an hour later.

"What did he say?" I asked.

"He didn't know what had gotten into you."

"Is he going home?"

"Yes."

All our unique walks with God can have strange twists and bumps. Mom and Dad were Christians who read their Bible regularly and attended church every Sunday. After witnessing all the fighting, adultery, and poverty, I can confirm that Jesus does not take away all suffering. Anyone who thinks that He does may be confused about His role in our lives.

The trials we experience shape and mold us in interesting and unique ways, but they are not easy to endure or to welcome. Still, in some crazy way, we are to "consider it pure joy ...whenever you face trials" (Jas. 1:2, NIV). These "trials" may be from many sources, like natural disasters, when we are sinned against, or even persecuted for living out our faith. Trials that come from other Christians, family members, and our close friends are the most challenging to endure. Finding joy in our trials can be an impossible task at times.

On one occasion, my father beat my mother so severely that he put her in the hospital. That was the only time he was ever put in jail for his actions. The rest of the time, the police, neighbors, friends, and even our pastor rarely intervened. I am sure he confessed his sins, however, his confession, and even his remorse, did not change the ugly consequences our family experienced as he violently enforced his rules and expectations on my mother.

When the trials in our lives are caused by a Christian who claims to live by and enforce God's law, it blinds one's ability to see God's love. The violence of the law is not for Christians to execute on others, yet if one lives by the law, consequences for sinning and breaking that law are necessitated. Christianity is about God's love, and it is certainly not about executing violence on others, especially in the way my father felt justified in punishing my mother for breaking his law. His actions were horrifying and unbalanced, and yet, are not all consequences condemning and painful? A Christians' trials should come from the world, which hates the truth of our salvation and is threatened by the love, and forgiveness Jesus showed us on the cross. Our suffering should not come from our self-condemnation or other Christians imposing rules and consequences on us.

My experiences, along with the scriptures I have shared, convinced me that a continual need to live under the law is a major contributor to the destruction in the lives of Christians. This cannot be what Jesus wanted. He didn't die on the cross so we could attempt to live by the law more effectively.

Under the law, once a standard of right is determined, others must be coerced into following this standard. If positive motivations do not work, guilt, confession, rebuke, forced repentance, judging, withholding love, violence, imprisonment, and death are all ways in which people may be negatively persuaded into following the standard. In my father's case, he could not stop enforcing what he believed was right, even when he repeatedly failed to forcefully conform my mother to his standards.

We can easily fall into the coercion trap of the law; therefore, it is crucial to understand how Jesus took away the law. He went to the cross to remove our sin and destruction, altering the religious status quo of how we live a *good life*. God pours His Spirit of love into our hearts, and, as we begin to emulate His forgiveness and sacrificial love, we are transformed. We no longer live by the law of sin and death, which depends on judgment and consequences. His Spirit's love in our hearts brings us new life in Christ Jesus. Jesus' work on the cross turned an upside-down world of judgment and condemnation, found through living by the law, into a *love-side-up* world of sacrificial and unconditional love, found through living by the way of the cross.

"Satan takes what is beautiful and ruins it; God takes what is ruined and makes it beautiful."[25] God's standard of beauty is love flowing from a person, not an outside standard of moral behavior, power, wealth, physical looks, and influence.

Practicing the love of Jesus allows us to be truly good to one another, even if the other person does not deserve it. This type of unconditional love does not come through obeying moral laws imposed by religion or tradition. Rules given by religion can make able people reasonable sinners, but only Jesus can make every one of us good. Religion is for "able people" because it only works for those who have the ability to keep its standards. To be truly "good" is to be a loving person made good by what Christ did on the cross, not by what we do. When my Christian, Bible-reading, church-attending father beat my mother, he might have thought of himself as a reasonable sinner, but he was not good. He attended church, repented, read the Bible, performed acts of service, and followed specific moral standards, but none of these actions made him good. To be good, he needed the love of Jesus to flow in him and through him. Jesus leads us to be loving and moral people but love comes first. My father did not need to be made a more legally righteous person by following a law; he needed to be made a more lovingly righteous person, worthy of being called good because he allowed the Spirit to teach him to love.

Aside from my tumultuous childhood, life has been relatively kind to me. I have enjoyed the wonders of education, marriage, building a family, owning property, and having various fulfilling jobs. Jesus has tremendously blessed me and all my needs are met. This is not to say that it has all come without struggle, but in the struggle, God has held me up in His love.

Even with God's love and blessings, I must constantly remember that money, power, being liked by the right people, and material possessions are not what will bring a *good life*. All these things can leave us empty and sometimes turn us into not-so-loving people. Peace and contentment in our lives are ultimately achieved by knowing and trusting in the love of Jesus. Abundant life is only found in living the way of the cross, not in the things the world promotes to bring a *good life*.

Most paths we choose purport to give us a sense of purpose and meaning, some lasting and some not. To have true and lasting meaning in life, we need a relationship with Jesus to guide us as we travel this road. We walk by the Spirit—God's heavenly guide of truth and love in our lives—with a blessed earthly purpose within the boundaries of that love.

When we choose to walk with God, we find He has an individual destiny for each of us, with a unique call and story. The darker side of my story is not necessarily worse than anyone else's. God has done many positive things in my life, and we all have tragedy and triumph in our stories. Although my father was an abusive husband, he somehow managed to be a decent parent. God will take each of our stories and make them beautiful works of art, even though some are more tragic and eventful than others. My story isn't intended to elicit pity or admiration. My life story was transformed into something beautiful because I participated in the work of Jesus Christ in me and began to seek His kingdom over my own. God has offered to make something special from each of our stories. He has called us to join His family and walk with Him, and He will help us succeed in incredible ways.

Chapter 16: Needed Repairs

Jesus was revealed to take away sins.

First John 3:5 (NET)

THE REALITY THAT CHRISTIANS struggle with sin seems a contradiction to the idea that Jesus took away our sins. Unfortunately, sin is a problem for everyone, not just for Christians. If sin is defined as breaking a rule, then none of us can avoid sinning—especially considering all of society's rules, religion's morals, government's laws, and the expectations of others. It's far to easy to commit minor or even major sins in our day-to-day interactions. These sins often require apologies, repentance, or even penance. Our transgression against another person may be so severe we cannot recover from the repercussions, making our physical presence no longer welcome. Even worse, people may find themselves in trouble with the police and the courts if they sin against the government's laws. Sin is a daily, moment-by-moment part of our lives because we have ample opportunities to fail at living according to the rules.

Often when we don't get it right, we receive the just desserts of our failures. Still, some individuals seem to get a free pass on the gravest of transgressions. If the justice and punishment we deserve do not manifest in this life, will it come in the next? The Bible contends that God has eternal consequences for our transgressions, and He will enforce justice in the afterlife for the unloving or evil behavior we perpetrate in this one (Rom. 9:27). Non-believers are promised punishment that justice would demand, and believers are promised removal of the evil that cannot be in the presence of God (2 Cor. 5:10).

In the early centuries of Christianity there were some interesting solutions to sanctify oneself from sin. One was the life of the ascetic: sheltering from society, living by a strict monastic code, and drastically limiting the pleasures of life. Beyond the blatant selfishness and self-achieved righteousness of this lifestyle, it appears they continued to have problems with sin. The book, *The Shepherd of Hermes*, written in the second century, is about a monk's temptation to lust after a nun. This detailed struggle with sin must have hit a chord with many people at the time since it was considered for the New Testament canon.

Another early ascetic, Evagrius Ponticus, is attributed to coming up with the list of the "eight principal vices."[26] In the following centuries, individuals like Pope Gregory I and St. Thomas Aquinas edited and elaborated on the list of vices to produce what eventually came to be known as the seven deadly sins: pride, greed, lust, envy, gluttony, anger, and laziness. To overcome these sins, followers were encouraged to exhibit "the seven corresponding virtues of humility, charity, chastity, gratitude, temperance, patience, and diligence."[27]

Is looking to the saints of the past the right way to define what sin is? What does the Bible say? The primary definition of the biblical word for "sin" is "missing the mark."[28] Most Christians understand missing the mark to mean failing to live up to God's law found in the Old Testament and failing to follow the New Testament's admonitions and prohibitions. As they seek to follow God and avoid sin, they are encouraged to search the scriptures to know what behaviors to avoid and what behaviors to emulate. A system of moral guidance is usually found by starting with a simple framework like the Ten Commandments and then selectively pulling from multiple biblical sources to add to the big ten. Christians generally agree on the appropriate core combination, but the peripheral sins vary from church to church.

When we label some sins as peripheral or less important, we are tempted to ask how close we can get to the less important sins without counting our actions as sinning. This is often referred to as living in gray areas. When I lived according to a list, frequently my internal motivations did not match my desired external moral behavior, forcing me to find a way to let my sin out. I would seek ways to skirt the rules, especially if it were a unique circumstance like a date with a dream girl or a night of revelry with the guys. I deserved to play outside the lines because I had behaved so well, according to my list. Living in gray areas can be dangerous because—unless our internal ideas of success correspond to our list of sins—in the wrong circumstances, our internal drives will bypass our list, and we will be left powerless to overcome our desires.

There are many seemingly benign activities that let Christians enjoy sin without sinning in the legal sense. These activities are often seen as a permissible and enjoyable way to cope with our struggles because it allows us to vent our darker side and seemingly prevents us from openly acting out our hidden desires. We may watch violent scenes and raunchy humor on television or in movies. We may join with evil while playing video games, magical dice, and fantasy card games. One's weakness may be reading edgy romance novels, or it might be joining in with the coarse talk at work. A common struggle among most people is a form of coveting. We watch endless improvement shows and videos, which lead us to desire a different house, better food, fancier vacations, nicer cars, connected friends, a more exciting career, and so on. While these types of shows on the things potentially available to us are innocent and fun, too much dwelling on what is superior to our current situation can lead to discontentment. Passively engaging in sins appears to be an attempt to vicariously experience the ways of the world while, at the same time, we can continue to profess our list as the way to achieve our sanctification. One's outside behavior may be perfected, but one's inner life is still in conflict (Matt. 23:28).

Living by a list of sins can profoundly affect how we treat ourselves and each other concerning judgment. When we discover and conquer a sin, do we keep it to ourselves or judge others by comparing their failure to our success? Our list can easily be used to judge and condemn ourselves, and it can turn us into a person who does the same to others, evoking guilt and shame. Beneficial guilt and shame can lead to change, but continual judgment combined with destructive guilt and shame can psychologically destroy one's mental stability.

A system of virtue allows the rule-keeper to see themselves as correct and to see those who disagree—or fail to keep the standards—as wrong.

Some Christians do not follow their own rules but tell themselves they are still better than those on the wrong side. "They are truly the evil in the world, not me." Rule-followers often give themselves a form of sanctity and self-righteousness by condemning anyone who disagrees with what they deem essential and moral issues. Despite the certainty of every Christian's eventual failure at keeping rules, feeling virtuous because of achievements according to standards can still prop up our feigned righteousness.

Overcoming sin through works of virtue and the ability to not transgress a list of rules gives us a status that puts us above a brother or sister who has not achieved the level of sinlessness that we have. This thinking tends to elevate believers to different levels of conquering sin. What level are we on? Not as high as our pastor but not as low as the church alcoholic, the person who went bankrupt, or the couple who failed at marriage. Self-righteousness can only lead to eventual disillusionment and empty pride because we cannot live up to our standards. When one's virtue is elevated, it becomes difficult for us to admit our failures publicly. Our pride, bolstered by the level of sinlessness we have assigned ourselves amongst the perceived bad behavior of others around us, gets in the way. There are indeed self-righteous pitfalls to having a legal system for overcoming sin, which negatively affects our relationship with God, others, and ourselves.

Unfortunately, teaching in the average church does not alleviate us from the idea of sin based on written standards. The church is more likely a place that points out the churchgoer's sin and promotes our attempts at ethical righteousness through our obedience to the law. When one inevitably fails to follow the prescribed rules, they are discouraged, and guilt is readily provided. They then are encouraged and instructed to fix their deviation through confession and repentance.

Teaching Christians to overcome sin by resolve, will, and self-denial is not what God wants either because it is living by our strength and conviction to abstain from a list of sins. I have seen people—who most would refer to as "mature Christians"—say and do some awful things in secret, which would be easily categorized as evil. When an admired Christian fails according to a law, it can feed into the religious practice of exposing the sin through confession and repentance or sometimes hiding the sin through denial and cover-up. All this guilt, repentance, and deception seems to function reasonably well by human effort, therefore it begs the question of God's role, especially when it involves institutional cover-up for the sake of a prominent Christian leader. Living by written standards of right and wrong does not seem to help us depend on and please the Holy Spirit, nor does it effectively rid us of sin.

When Christians define sin as failing to follow the law or "missing the mark," they are not embracing the new freedom we have in Christ. When living by moral rules defining sins, we are slaves to the sins that the rules define. As imperfect humans, even with our greatest effort, we will fail to hit the mark consistently and fall under the law's condemnation. At some point in our lives, we may achieve a level of accuracy, but these times are quickly fading. When we miss it, no one cares how often we hit it. Even when we are spiritual, acting holy, or following a set of morals, we are most likely doing it by our own effort, which also misses the mark.

What hits the mark is a belief in the work that Christ accomplished on the cross as the perfect, spotless Lamb who worked to repair the destruction of sin in our lives and to restore our relationship with God. The sacrificial lamb of the Old Testament law only covered sins for temporary communion with God. The perfect Lamb of God took away our sins permanently (1 John 3:5; John 1:29) to restore our lost relationship with the creator forever. What we cannot and could not fix, Christ can and already did on the cross. God has taken away our sins according to the law and restored us to a sinless state so we can walk with Him in a loving relationship.

Understanding the experiential truth of Jesus taking away our sins (1 John 3:5) requires us to embrace the concept that the believer should no longer attempt to live the Christian life by avoiding sins delineated by the Mosaic law, New Testament passages, or anywhere else. To take away our sins, Jesus had to eradicate the instrument of condemnation. We should no longer perceive sin as delineated by the Old Testament law because God is not using a list to define transgressions between Him and us. Sin, especially according to a list, no longer separates us from God. Sadly, lists of sins are used very successfully as a tool to control us, condemn us, and make us feel separated from God and our fellow believers. Lists of sins will always overwhelm us and enslave us.

Paul goes to great lengths in Romans to explain our freedom from sin. He wrote that, under the law, we are slaves to what we obey (Rom. 6:16). When we hold on to rules to define sin, we eventually will be forced to choose a means of coping with the struggle between the law and our sin. This choice takes two forms. First, we may attempt to obey the law and become a slave to fighting sin. Second, we may rebel against the law and allow sin to rule, fully indulging in destructive behavior.

When Paul wrote that we "are not under Law but under grace" (Rom. 6:14, NASB), he expounded on the magnitude of Jesus' removal of our sins. Since we are no longer under the Mosaic law, sin cannot be disobeying a law we are no longer obligated to follow (Rom. 6:14–15). Logically speaking, how can Christians sin according to the law if Jesus has taken away the law delineating their sins? The only way to have sinned according to a written law is to transgress the law, but the law no longer applies to the believer.

Romans 7 is commonly thought of as Paul's personal experience of the Christian's struggle with sin and law as a believer. While Paul did indeed describe the sin conflict and the role of law, it is for a higher purpose. He explains how it is impossible to live a pure life by following the law, even for a Christian.

Paul demonstrates how the law stirs up and points out our sin, making us powerless to overcome it: "For while we were in the flesh, the sinful passions, which were aroused by the Law, were at work in the members of our body to bear fruit for death" (Rom. 7:5, NASB). Our struggle with sin and the law is only overcome when we turn to Jesus to rescue us from our slavery to sin, which is partially caused by the law.

When someone is a slave to sin and in a state of rebellion, they disregard the requirements of the law and sometimes intentionally do the opposite. Their hearts may become wicked and evil, seeking whom they can devour. A person can become bent on destruction, looking to steal, kill, or destroy to get their needs met. If they do not develop shame and remorse, they may develop a passion for destroying those who condemn them. Their sin and passion can become insatiable without restraint, and they may begin to take advantage of others in grotesque ways. They become slaves to sin and bear its destruction.

It may be easy to see how irresponsible living keeps us in a state of enslavement to sin. yet it can be a little harder to understand that a significant amount of Christian teaching keeps us in a state of being controlled by sin, promoting the struggle to overcome it. This is fostered by the belief that struggling with sin, defined by the law, is the right path for the Christian life. Paul would contend that one who defines sin by the law is not free from sin and the law; that individual still lives under its curse. Keeping the focus on sin according to a list of laws keeps one in bondage to sin and makes sin the issue our master. When bound by the law, we find ourselves continually attempting to find ways to live according to our knowledge of good and evil, which leaves us unable to freely and fully experience the *good life* that God's love brings.

The life of struggle with the law and sin, which had a stranglehold on people's lives, can be set aside. "But now we have been released from the Law, having died to that by which we were bound, so that we serve in newness of the Spirit and not in oldness of the letter" (Rom. 7:6, NASB). Sin has no power over us when we walk in the Spirit and follow Jesus' love as our guide to being sanctified. If we walk according to the law—or any moral or religious rules—we are under another power, and we can quickly become a slave to sin, living as if our sins are not taken away.

Despite our freedom from sin defined by biblical laws, there is an ongoing tension between our complete freedom in Christ, with our sin no longer delineated by written rules, and a world that functions entirely by rules. Rightly so, one might strongly contend that we need written laws to constrain our behavior, even if we are made new by the Spirit. Government laws, religious practices, family rules, and cultural pressures to conform often effectively change designated outside behavior, but what about changing a person's desires on the inside? It is a noble goal to fix a person's behavior, yet seeing their core motivation change, where they are led by the Spirit to show the love of Jesus, is a change on a higher level. No written law defining sin can come close to bringing a love-based change in one's life like the Spirit wants to do in every believer.

When one approaches sin delineated by a list of rules, they are judging according to that written standard instead of living by the grace given at the cross. When living by grace, sin becomes not trusting God and not learning to love as Jesus loves when led and taught by the Spirit. This understanding reflects the "meat" of the gospel versus the "milk" that the apostle Paul wrote of (1 Cor. 3:1–3). When we live by the Spirit, we do not start with condemnation but with complete acceptance despite our failures. This does not give us a license to do whatever we want because the Spirit lets us know when we fail to love with the love of the cross. Sins, defined by rules, are taken away, and we are afforded the opportunity to live in the Spirit's grace, love, and guidance.

It then stands to reason that since written sins between us and God are taken away, we should strive to have no law between our brothers and sisters in Christ except the law of the Spirit. For the believer, while we still have endless earthly obligations and countless opportunities to sin according to worldly rules, we are meant to experience the new reality of living by the Spirit. We are free from the law and seek to live and love as He guides us, without needing a list of sins for "...against such things there is not law." (Gal. 5:23b, NET).

What about all the lists of rules in the New Testament? A life lived by the Spirit is hard to realize and participate in if we still cannot let go of using the Bible for a list of sins and admonitions as the path to being sanctified. Learning to live by the Spirit is drawing closer to Jesus and learning to love in place of rules, not learning more rules so we do not sin. Without this understanding, we will read the Bible with blinders on, looking for rules to live by. This does not mean we don't love and cherish all that the Bible says. All scripture is necessary to know the truth concerning God and salvation, good and evil, darkness and light, truth and falsehood, and what is loving and hateful (2 Tim. 3:16). Embracing the significant role of Scripture in our lives does not change the fact that being righteous based on the knowledge of good and evil has never been what God wanted for us. He wants the same thing He has always wanted: to be our God, walk in a relationship with us, and teach us to love.

Even with the Spirit perfecting us in Christ's love, we will still never be fully perfected in the flesh. We can and do commit unloving acts toward God, others, and ourselves. We can be lazy mistake-makers who lose our temper when we don't get our way. We find it difficult to control our lust for money, lust for food, lust for sex, lust for what someone else has, and lust to live a life of pleasure. We may be tempted to indulge ourselves at the expense of others. Even if we have victory over the flesh, we can still quickly fall into darkness with a flash of anger, a glance of lust, or a rush of envy in our hearts. Believers can cause problems and destruction to the point of ruining their witnesses and sometimes ending their lives.

Our dark actions are not done solely by the entity called our flesh, for we are whole beings. These deeds are not enacted by an outside force called sin; if a force exists, it is given power by our own evil fleshly desires. Our lousy behavior consists of volitionary actions we take, whether we have the strength to resist or not. But be forewarned; you cannot bring your darkness and evil with you in the next life to be with Jesus. Living in darkness, or even living by a written law to stop sinning, is the opposite of being motivated by God's Spirit of love in us. Remember, our sanctification is not about how little we sin according to fleshly rules but how much we love, led by the Spirit.

One scripture passage that helps us understand the struggle with darkness is First Corinthians 10:1-13.

> "For I do not want you to be unaware, brothers and sisters, that our fathers were all under the cloud and all passed through the sea, and all were baptized into Moses in the cloud and in the sea, and all ate the same spiritual food, and all drank the same spiritual drink. For they were all drinking from the spiritual rock that followed them, and the rock was Christ. But God was not pleased with most of them, for they were cut down in the wilderness. These things happened as examples for us, so that we will not crave evil things as they did. So do not be idolaters, as some of them were. As it is written, "The people sat down to eat and drink and rose up to play." And let us not be immoral, as some of them were, and twenty-three thousand died in a single day. And let us not put Christ to the test, as some of them did, and were destroyed by snakes. And do not complain, as some of them did, and were killed by the destroying angel. These things happened to them as examples and were written for our instruction, on whom the ends of the ages have come. So let the one who thinks he is standing

be careful that he does not fall. No trial has overtaken you that is not faced by others. And God is faithful: He will not let you be tried beyond what you are able to bear, but with the trial will also provide a way out so that you may be able to endure it."

(NET)

We are all familiar with verse 13, implying we can overcome temptation, but we are less familiar with the temptations Paul lists in verses 6 through 10. He walks his readers through the categorical downfalls of the Children of Israel in the desert. Paul uses this list to warn believers of the behavior that will destroy their lives. He calls them a desire "of evil things." These are things contrary to love and they appease our desires in the wrong way. The first "evil thing," he states, is idolatry. Idolatry implies something we depend upon for our ultimate salvation. It could be worshiping other gods, money, science, education, strength, family, or governments, any of these. The second is sexual immorality, which is a sexual act or a physical relationship outside a lifelong marriage between a man and a woman. Next is putting "Christ to the test." It is being discontent with the circumstances God has placed us in and trying to force Him to fix it for us. Adding on to this, Paul insists that we do not complain. We all know how destructive constant complaining can be. It's like a negative attitude on a sports team or in an office; it will ruin the morale. (1 Cor. 10:6-10, NET)

When Paul says the law is dead, he is fully aware that actions and thoughts exist that will harm you and possibly destroy your life. The new covenant teaches a new path of living a life of truth and love, guided by the Spirit. This new way negates the need for the law, and the temptations to "crave evil things" can be overcome because ". . . God is faithful: He will not let you be tried beyond what you are able to bear, but with the trial will also provide a way out so that you may be able to endure it." (1 Cor. 10:13b, NET)

By the power of the Spirit in us, we can choose to walk in the light—or by our flesh, we can choose to walk in darkness. We can choose to love or choose to hate. We can choose to love the things of the world or choose to despise the things of the world and seek the things of God. We can choose to take advantage of others, using them to build our esteem, for our sexual pleasure, financial success, or to improve our position in life, or we can choose to live the way of the cross and to love others sacrificially.

The final truth in our struggle to realize that Jesus has taken away our sins is that God will not even judge the believer's worthiness to be saved by how much they failed to love, although we know that is extremely important to Him. All written laws defining sin and condemnation are removed based on one's belief in Jesus. This revolutionary transformation happens at the very moment in time when we choose to believe and follow Him (John 5:24). That decision is the foundation of the *good life* Jesus promises. Subsequently, our understanding that Jesus took away our sins, along with the written law, builds on that foundation by participating with the Holy Spirit to live a life free from sin. The ultimate sin, the one that separates you from a *good life*, which is free from the condemnation of sin in the here and now and the final condemnation that will separate you from God for all eternity, is the sin of unbelief (John 3:18, 36).

Chapter 17: Miraculously Fixed

For God did not send his Son into the world to condemn the world, but that the world should be saved through him.

John 3:17 (NET)

SALVATION IN JESUS has taken me leaps and bounds towards the *good life*. I am forgiven and free from sins, justified to be in God's presence, adopted as His child, and filled with His Spirit. Even with all these blessings, it seems that not a day goes by that I am not reminded of my wrongs. I can easily be overtaken by a depressing thought of past failures, a passing comment by others, or a feeling of loss from a missed opportunity gone by. How can I not feel condemnation?

It's difficult to actualize the life-changing implications of the cross in our present reality because it takes away all our sins and ends our obligation to the law. In doing this, it removed all condemnation for the believer. In Paul's gospel presentation in his letter to the Romans, after his lengthy opine in chapter seven about how overcoming sin through living by the law is impossible, he climaxes in chapter eight by exclaiming the truth about how we are free from the condemnation of the law when we are in Jesus:

> There is therefore now no condemnation for those who are in Christ Jesus. For the law of the life-giving Spirit in Christ Jesus has set you free from the law of sin and death.
>
> Romans 8:1–2(NET)

During my senior year in college, I had the privilege of rooming with a Rwandan student, Rev. Major Charles Deogratias. He was tall, sophisticated and had a great sense of pride in his heritage, along with his zeal for Jesus. His striking personality was in stark contrast to the fact that Charles had been raised in a refugee camp in Tanzania. It appeared that his positive demeanor flowed from the miracle of Jesus saving him and providing a path to come halfway around the world to get a degree in ministry at a Christian university. It has been over thirty years but I still vividly remember his constant quoting of Romans 8:1 (CSB), "Therefore, there is now no condemnation for those in Christ Jesus." He must have said it at least once every time he saw me. Maybe he perceived that I did not live by grace but instead focused on the law and the condemnation I felt for myself. It was not until years later that I understood my African brother's obsession with this verse.

Romans 8:1 is maybe the greatest truth about the gospel that the apostle Paul penned. It is the pivotal point in his complex and thorough explanation of the gospel. He explodes with his climax that we have no condemnation because we have been set free from a life of sin and death according to the law. We are set free to make any choice we want without any threat of condemnation. Paul knew that, in Christ, we could be completely free because the same power that sets us free also leads us to make good and loving decisions concerning those around us. Our freedom from the law and condemnation came from the one who demonstrated the greatest example of sacrificial love. He then gave us the Spirit to empower us to live this freedom in Christ's love.

Paul begins his climactic chapter with his bold statement of no condemnation and he ends it with his life-changing, religion-destroying proclamation that nothing "will be able to separate us from the love of God that is in Christ Jesus our Lord" (Rom. 8:39, NIV). The prescribed sins given by religion certainly cannot separate us from God. God is love, and in Him, there is no sin (1 John 3:9). Therefore, if we are in God, He is in us, and His love is in us, we can be completely free from the grips of sin, and therefore, nothing can separate us from God (1 John 3:9, 4:7–8). We have the possibility of no sin because we are not under an old covenant of laws, rewards, and punishments. We are under a new covenant of living by the

Spirit, and no law is left to define a sin that would condemn or separate us from Him.

Teaching that we must obey God according to rules and that we will be punished when we do wrong and rewarded when we do right is the "carrot and stick"[29] argument, as Aaron Budjen labels it. This approach makes Christians feel separated from God when they trangress, and some even think they have lost their salvation. Conditional blessing is also how the Jews in Jesus' day perceived God's interactions with humans. The disciples illustrated this when they saw a blind man and asked Jesus, "Who sinned, this man or his parents, that he was born blind?" (John 9:2, NKJV). It is often insinuated that bad things happen to us because we are out of the will of God, which seems to be a form of Christian karma. That is not how a loving Father treats His children.

This mindset of condemnation is created by continuing to live by the law of sin and death and it keeps us on a rollercoaster of uncertainty. Instead, by faith in what Jesus accomplished on the cross, we should be free to live by the Spirit in truth and love with no threat of condemnation. Knowing true and permanent forgiveness sets us free from a life controlled by sin, and it will most certainly set us free from the fear of separation from God to live a new, unique, and uninhibited life in Jesus, guided by the Spirit.

Strangely enough, I have found that even those who believe in total grace, with only the commandment to love, still have hidden taboo sins. It seems some hold the thought in the back of their minds: What is the one thing that I could do that would destroy my relationship with God and maybe end my forgiveness? I know that practitioners of grace say they do not believe such a taboo trespass exists, but deep down, fear of judgment for committing a forbidden sin can still haunt us. For the believer, this belief in a drastic sin should not exist. No sin, except the sin of unbelief, before we know Jesus, separates us from God's love (Rom. 8:39) or summons God's condemnation (Rom. 8:1-2). Complete forgiveness, spiritual blessings, and unending love are not compatible with belief in some sort of condemnation for a sin like suicide or murder. Jesus took away all fear of an unforgivable sin when He took away the old covenant and instituted righteousness through belief.

This is not to say that we do not feel and receive condemnation from others and ourselves. It can come from all sides, especially when we act against our church community rules. We also experience judgment from the world if we commit any action that they deem immoral. We face increased condemnation from unbelievers because of their preconceived beliefs about what Christians should and should not do. Even our families, Christian or not, will scorn us if we offend established family traditions. Sadly, we even condemn ourselves for our mistakes and can be highly judgmental of our person regarding our actions.

There is also a supernatural aspect to the condemnation we feel. Satan is the worst source of condemnation in our lives. He works to condemn us using all of the above sources and more if given a chance. God calls Satan: "The accuser of our brothers and sisters, who accuses them before our God day and night" (Rev. 12:10, NIV). It is hopeful to know that someday we will be completely free from condemnation from others, ourselves, and even Satan.

In the new covenant, with our only commandment being to love as Jesus loved, one may find a reason for self-condemnation in their failure to show this love. While we can easily become estranged from one another's love, we cannot become estranged from God's love. Any wrong we have done has already been paid for, and we are completely forgiven by Him and are continually in fellowship with God (1 John 1:7, 9; Rom. 8:39). He will not wrathfully discipline us each time we get it wrong, nor will God leave us alone until we get it right (Heb. 13:5–6). His Spirit will correct our unloving behavior and lead us to the loving behavior He desires for us (Rom. 8:26; 2 Tim. 1:7; Gal. 5:16, 25). Again, our "sin" does not change God's love toward us. However, our "sin" may change our hearts and blind us to the Spirit's work in and through us, but that is not the same as God's condemning or breaking fellowship (Heb. 6:4–6).

Knowing that God does not practice condemnation against believers, I am compelled not to practice condemnation against others or myself, especially my siblings in Christ. Can I love someone and condemn them at the same time? Maybe as an appointed parent, boss, or public office holder, but not as a brother, sister, or friend. We should afford the same grace to one another as God affords to us (Phil. 2:1–6).

The paradigm shift, from a life of bondage and condemnation under the law to a life of freedom in the Spirit, is so mind-wrecking that most of us fail to understand it, even after Paul spends eight chapters explaining it in his letter to the Romans. Jesus' act on the cross has forgiven us, healed us (Col. 1:14; 1 John 1:9; Acts 26:18), and made a way for His Spirit to live in us (Rom. 8:2). His love has overwhelmed us (Rom. 8:39), and our adoption has given us a whole new life and destiny (Rom. 8:29–30). We live a blessed life as children of God the Father (1 John 3:1; Rom. 8:15–17). In addition to all of these amazing gifts, gaining a grasp of the amazing fact that the cross takes away all of our sin and condemnation (1 John 3:5; Rom. 8:2), further transforms and enriches our experience of the *good life* God promised.

Chapter 18: Routine Maintenance

"Blessed are those whose lawless deeds are forgiven, and whose sins are covered; blessed is the one against whom the Lord will never count sin."

Romans 4:7-8 (NET)

BECOMING A CHRISTIAN does not make us sinless in the flesh; no one has discovered a bulletproof way to live a life of love with no mistakes. There are some significant differences in the way Christians respond when they fail. These differences hinge on how we believe God responds to our failures and what He expects us to do about them.

In the last chapter, I attempted to explain our freedom from condemnation. If we believe the goal is to be holy according to rules, and when we sin, God breaks fellowship with us and we must subsequently confess to restore that fellowship, we are practicing a system of condemnation. Insistence on confession to fix our estrangement does not fit with Paul's declarations that we have no condemnation and that there is nothing we can do that will separate us from God's love.

Confession is widely practiced to receive perceived forgiveness for our sins. It is hard for people to give up confession as a means of petitioning God to alleviate their trespasses. Even if one understands it is misguided to not fully acknowledge their complete forgiveness given at the cross, they may still hold that the confession commanded in First John 1:9 is for restoring our relationship with God. In either case, forgiveness or restoration, confession is thought necessary to fix our broken relationship between God and us.

Let's take a deeper look at First John 1:9 in its broader context since it is the central passage used to promote the idea of the ongoing Christian confession of sins:

> 6. If we say we have fellowship with him and yet keep on walking in the darkness, we are lying and not practicing the truth. 7. But if we walk in the light as he himself is in the light, we have fellowship with one another and the blood of Jesus his Son cleanses us from all sin. 8. If we say we do not bear the guilt of sin, we are deceiving ourselves and the truth is not in us. 9. But if we confess our sins, he is faithful and righteous, forgiving us our sins and cleansing us from all unrighteousness. 10. If we say we have not sinned, we make him a liar and his word is not in us.
>
> First John 1:6–10 (NET)

In verses six and seven, a situation occurs when one claims, as I do, that a believer does not sin by transgressing the Mosaic law or by failing to do a prescribed good. We are left with a question: How do I know right behavior? The answer given is to walk in the Spirit (Gal. 5:16). But what does that look like? John and Paul both describe this new journey as walking in the light and not walking in darkness (1 John 1:6–7, Col. 1:12–13). John goes on in the later chapters of First John to juxtapose love versus hate, which corresponds to the light and darkness analogy (1 John 2:9–11). Walking in the light is walking by the Spirit in His freedom, truth, and love, knowing we are fully cleansed from all unrighteousness (1 John 1:9). We can live free from sin, which enslaves us to the temptations of the darkness of this world, and live free from law, which enslaves us to a religious system.

Verse eight explains how we will struggle to stay in His light, and that we often sin by missing the goal of loving as Jesus loved. A forgiven person should have no hindrances in openly admitting their failure to love when someone else points it out. Don't worry—people will readily point out our problems. Generally, we do not need others to convict us because we often see our own failures, most likely with the Spirit's prompting. Our willingness to openly accept and confess our failures should not lead to overwhelming guilt and shame, instead it should lend to humility and curiosity about how to do it better next time.

Verse nine teaches that everyone fails to love as Jesus loves, and therefore sins. When we fail, confessing our sins is extremely important in helping us know the truth and hope of the forgiveness Jesus has already provided. Confession is also part of the process of pruning[30] (cleansing) us of any hindrances[31] to loving (unrighteousness) and teaching us to demonstrate God's love (righteousness). When we acknowledge our failure to love God or to love one another, we are spurred on to love well in the future according to the grace we have received.

In verse ten, we see that no law can lift us to the perfect eternal height of Jesus' love; only His Spirit in us can lead us closer to His likeness. Sanctification by right living according to rules, achieved in our own strength, only leads us to the darkness of hiding or denying our unloving behavior, often contending "that we have not sinned."

Reaching an admired level of practical sanctification can put us in a place where we think we no longer need the Spirit of God to make us more loving. How many of us have been hurt by someone who was considered a highly spiritual and moral person in the church? Failure to love by Christian leadership has caused deep wounding. No one is past walking in the darkness; I would guess the apostle John even failed at times. When we think we are too good to fail, we "make Him a liar, and His word is not in us."

Human tendency to obfuscate our mistakes is why John reiterates in verses six, eight, and ten that when we deny our failings, we make God out to be a liar. We are often tempted to not admit our wrongs because we fear condemnation and harm from others. For understandable reasons, my mother almost always denied any activity my father angrily accused her of. It became a reflex for her to deny accusations of wrongdoing in the face of his judgment and condemnation. An open willingness to confess and not to deny when we fail to love, vastly differs from the general procedure of confession when we sin according to a rule and then face dire consequences. One is done out of love and the other is done out of fear. Confession out of love and not fear is the way of Jesus because we know "there is no fear in love" (1 John 4:18, NASB).

Simply stated, if we are confessing anything but our failure to love as Jesus loved, we are professing commandments or rules we transgressed. This results in using written rules by which we condemn ourselves and often others.

The way we behave towards others often reflects how we see God relates to us. I shared with you about the fights between my mother and father to illustrate what extreme judging and condemning others looks like. Embedded in their arguments were my father's futile attempts to get my mother to admit her wrongs, most likely to justify his hurt, anger, and violence. He wanted her confession to make things right, although it would not have worked because of his brokenness. He was not the only Christian I have met with this dark side of judgment and condemnation in their life. Although most don't go around punishing others physically, they still demand repentance and confession and have other ways of doling out consequences.

Having our righteousness based on our faith in what God did and does for us, means our forgiveness is solely based on our decision to have a relationship with Jesus, not whether we have confessed all or most of our sins. Our sanctification is not achieved through confession and good behavior; that description sounds more like a method of receiving parole from a prison term than a loving relationship with a Father who adopted us as His children.

I am aware that a majority of Christians would disagree. Most still define sin as breaking a rule, not failing to love. If rules define sin, our confession then is for forgiveness from the identified sins that keep us from God. While some might differentiate between accidental and willful sins, it is still virtually impossible to remember and acknowledge all our sins—this results in us throwing up a blanket confession for all the sins we were unaware of. The weakness of this argument is found in the question, "When are we law-abiding and all of our sins confessed?" The honest answer is "never." In a system of sanctification by works and confession, there seems to be no end to discovering sins to confess. If we have never fully confessed everything, then we can never have full fellowship with God and complete forgiveness.

Another passage used to support the idea of loss of fellowship is found in Ephesians: "Do not grieve the Holy Spirit of God" (Eph. 4:30, NKJV). Does grieving the Holy Spirit cause us to lose fellowship in the sense of separation?

If my daughter commits an offensive act toward me, we may have words, but she is still my daughter. I do not stop loving her, and she does not stop loving me. I would grieve if my daughter stopped loving me and communicated this to me, but it would not change my love for her. If she abandoned Jesus and lived a destructive life, this would grieve me too, yet I would still love her. My grief would not be against her; it would be for what she is losing by her choice.

God grieves for the loss and destruction we bring into our lives through our bad choices. He does not separate Himself from us with His grief; He cries for us and with us. We are not condemned, we do not lose our forgiveness, and we still have our relationship with our Father, regardless of the offense (Rom. 8:38–39).

The threat of lost fellowship with God should not exist for the believer. Loss of fellowship may come from convincing ourselves that we must confess all our sins as the key to having fellowship. John later wrote that if "our heart condemns us, God is greater than our heart" (1 John 3:20, NKJV). We may feel out of fellowship, but God's open arms have not changed. He does not stare at us with crossed arms and a scowl on His face, waiting for us to return with our tail between our legs, confessing and repenting our sins. Nor does He hand out treats with a happy face to those who do not mess up or to those who are genuinely repentant and confess with sincerity. God is a good Father who stands with open arms to love us, despite what we have done or whether we confess correctly. He is like the Father in Jesus' story of the prodigal son. The father rejoices that his son has returned, despite all of the evil he has done. He does not wait for his son to repent, he rejoices at the moment he sees him coming towards him, not even knowing the pretense or the outcome of his return. He even rebukes his good son for demanding justice be served on the evil brother. The picture of a loving father running to greet his wayward son is such a profound illustration of the love of God in a Christian's life, and it demonstrates that His love will not go away, despite what we do (Luke 13:11–32).

Continuing to believe that we must resolve our separation from God by confessing our sin does not fix our relationship with Him, nor does it resolve our sin problem (Heb. 10:29). This thinking and practice causes self-condemnation, which separates us from His love in our hearts and minds

(Heb. 6:4–6), Christ did not go to the cross to re-establish the religious practice of confession of sin to receive forgiveness or restored fellowship. He went to the cross to end the confession of transgressions of laws by completely changing the way we define and deal with sin. "For sin shall no longer be your master, because you are not under the law, but under grace" (Rom. 6:14, NIV).

It is true that a believer's sin would get in the way of having fellowship with God; that is why God has removed our sins and given us complete forgiveness. Why are we confessing our sins to receive forgiveness if we already have complete forgiveness? Are we trying to duplicate what Jesus has already accomplished on the cross (Heb. 10:29)? The forgiveness of the cross sets us free from the need to confess our sins to alleviate our condemnation since our transgressions are completely forgiven at salvation, past, present, and future.

This does not mean we do not confess our failures. In our walk with Jesus, we will inevitably fail at times to love with His love. Since we have already received the transforming effect of His complete love and forgiveness, we are empowered to confess to each other because we have nothing to fear. As God is perfecting His love in us, a willingness to openly admit our failures to one another is a substantial part of learning to love as Jesus loves.

In light of this need to confess to one another, we should not take John's admonition to confess lightly. We must fully embrace it with the understanding that sin is a failure to love. If we have failed at love, we should openly confess to others and freely talk to God about our transgression. This is a process of letting God cleanse us of our unloving ways (1 John 1:9). Our confession is not made out of fear, guilt, shame, and a need to restore a relationship with God; it is made out of a desire to be perfected in God's love and to repair relationships with others. It's not a confession out of fear because the cross transformed the practice of confession by transforming the Christian's definition of sin with the institution of the new covenant.

Our bold ability to confess our failures exists because there is nothing that can separate us from God's forgiveness and love. When we fail to love another person, the appropriate response is almost always to apologize, confess, and not deny our wrongdoing. Denial of our failures would be the opposite of confession. Ideally, we strive never to deny or hide our lack of love—nor should we have any reason to do so—because we are unconditionally loved and not condemned by God. The Spirit will help us to decipher the most loving action, which is usually openly confessing our failures to each other (Jas. 5:16). Again, it is essential to know that God's love has not changed towards us when we fail. Our relationship with Him is never broken, so confession to God is not mandated for His forgiveness (Rom. 8:39). We are not even separated from God by our failure to love; therefore, no action on our part would rescind the forgiveness of the cross nor our ability to meet with God in the fullness of His love.

The ultimate hope is that as we grow closer to being perfected in His love, the possibility of hateful and evil acts will grow further away from us. Discussions with God and others about bad or unfortunate behavior should be done without fearing separation from God (1 John 4:18). In a perfect world, others would not condemn us either. We can come to God to confess in a spirit of thankfulness for His unending love and sorrow for not listening to Him or not practicing love as the Spirit led us.

Bathed in the Father's great love and forgiveness, and motivated by our desire to love as Jesus loved us, we are free to openly confess to God and one another when we sin by failing to love well. This freedom is key to allowing God's Spirit to work in and transform us. An open, humble, and trusting conversation with God and others allows Him to change us as we are shown our shortcomings in our attempts to love. Hopefully, as we mature in our faith, our conversations will not continue to be about what we have done wrong but about what we are doing right.

Chapter 19: Backing Up When We Make a Wrong Turn

Then Peter came to Him and said, "Lord, how often shall my brother sin against me, and I forgive him? Up to seven times?" Jesus said to him, "I do not say to you, up to seven times, but up to seventy times seven."

Matthew 18:21-22 (NKJV)

AS I STOOD WITH MY mother at the side of my father's casket, I held back tears long enough to ask her if she forgave him. Even though he deeply loved her, he was verbally and physically abusive for most of their marriage. Since she had recently suffered from a stroke, she could only nod and utter a faint noise resembling a "yes," or at least I thought that's what she said. Some aspects of my life were challenging to face because I had held onto my unforgiveness towards my father for his abuse of my mother. My moment with Mom at the casket was a step in the right direction.

A given in this life is that broken people break others. My father hurt me, my mother, and my family with his violence and anger. My mother was also broken and let me down countless times. Their failures were my life's first and most impacting causes of harm, but of course, more would come. I have been judged harshly, lied about, taken advantage of, and even rejected at times by my family, friends, and the church. More than I would like, I find myself clinging to trespasses instead of forgiving and forgetting. I keep a record of wrongs and withhold forgiveness arbitrarily. I readily understand

I must extend forgiveness to many people in daily interactions––the more difficult task is recognizing when I hurt others and need their forgiveness.

My wife and I got stuck on a high mountain four-wheel drive road while she was nine months pregnant with our first child. On our daring adventure, we drove up to a sign that read: "Passengers Walk / Certain Death." It didn't look that bad to me but she insisted on getting out while I drove across. I quickly ascertained the reason for the sign. As I maneuvered over a large rock, lifting the front left tire, it forcefully sent my right rear tire off the road, potentially down the hill to destruction. My saving grace was a bar someone had cemented in place to catch the back wheel, foregoing drivers from the worst day of their lives or maybe the last. I can only wonder who put it there. How many naïve explorers had previously tried and failed at this problem?

That wasn't the end of our troubles. Just a way further, around the bend, the road was covered by a landslide of shale rock. Instead of making it over the pass, we had to reverse a hairpin corner, turn the truck around in an impossible circumstance, and re-navigate the "Passengers Walk / Certain Death" problem.

It stretched both of us to our very wits end. Did I mention my wife was nine months pregnant, and we were in a king cab, long-bed truck? Fortunately, we made it out alive and relatively unscathed. The traumatic incident sobered me up about making better decisions to keep my wife and child safe, and even though we managed to survive unharmed, my wife has never trusted me to take her off-roading again.

The reckless adventure was an unfortunate lapse in judgment, but it would not be the last, and not even close to the worst mistake I would make. The list just kept piling up. Each one had the potential of certain death in our marriage––I was continually almost rolling down the hill. My wife has not permanently exited the truck, but I'm sure it has crossed her mind. Even though we seem to work through it all, it still lingers, just like we never go off-roading. I try to believe that God can fix and heal us, but it never seems to be entirely resolved. It's just not that simple.

Marriage is a fitting object lesson in understanding forgiveness. A bad marriage can result in constant judgment and condemnation based on past failures and performances. A great marriage can be an excellent model of forgiveness, where grace is shown in almost every circumstance because love keeps no record of wrongs. In my experience and observation of mine and other relationships, this level of forgiveness is a supernatural requirement. It's the forgiveness that Christ modeled for us, but can we live it? Without forgiveness, every act of love will become tainted by what was broken. With forgiveness, we can love again with sincerity, despite past sins and the knowledge of our inevitable future failures.

How then is life lived with forgiveness? How do we back around hairpin curves? How do we navigate our mistakes in an unforgiving world? Without Jesus to catch us, I have no answers. Circumstances in life are complex, and people often do not respond the way we expect them to. When we make mistakes, we can't predict the outcome. No matter how hard we try to fix things, we may fail miserably, and everything can go wrong. Depending on each other's forgiveness and hoping somehow to make it through the problem together, does not always work. In the end, the only solution may be to take our broken and mistake-filled self and place it in His hands so we can get back on the road. We will fail but He will catch us, like the bar caught me.

Christians are to seek to forgive in the likeness of the cross out of gratitude for what has been done for them. Matthew recounts a story Jesus told about a king who forgives a large debt. The receiver of that favor turns around and refuses to forgive someone who owes him a small amount of money.

> For this reason, the kingdom of heaven is like a king who wanted to settle accounts with his slaves. As he began settling his accounts, a man who owed ten thousand talents was brought to him. Because he was not able to repay it, the Lord ordered him to be sold, along with his wife, children, and whatever he possessed, and repayment to be made. Then the slave threw himself to the ground before him, saying, 'Be patient with me, and I will repay you everything.' The Lord had compassion on that slave and released him, and forgave him the debt. After he went out, that same slave found one of his fellow slaves who owed him one hundred silver coins. So he grabbed him by the throat and started to choke him, saying, 'Pay back what you owe me!' Then his fellow

slave threw himself down and begged him, 'Be patient with me, and I will repay you.' But he refused. Instead, he went out and threw him in prison until he repaid the debt. When his fellow slaves saw what had happened, they were very upset and went and told their Lord everything that had taken place. Then his Lord called the first slave and said to him, 'Evil slave! I forgave you all that debt because you begged me! Should you not have shown mercy to your fellow slave, just as I showed it to you?' And in anger his Lord turned him over to the prison guards to torture him until he repaid all he owed. So also my heavenly Father will do to you, if each of you does not forgive your brother from your heart.

> Matthew 18:23–35 (NET)

In this parable, we find comfort when the large debt is forgiven and are immediately incensed at the thought that the person forgiven would not forgive another for a far lesser debt. This parable is even more poignant for believers. While those without Jesus will suffer after death for their cruelty and unforgiveness in this world, we as believers will not. If we have been forgiven so much, why would we not freely forgive others?

Jesus makes an even more profound point. He implies being forgiven does not make everyone a better person. Forgiveness did not work in the wicked man's life because it is not a magic wand, but it should work for those who believe and choose to follow Jesus.

The great forgiveness the king demonstrated is found at the cross: "But God demonstrates his own love for us in this: While we were still sinners, Christ died for us" (Rom. 5:8, NIV). Jesus suffered on the cross while we still actively caused destruction. The love Jesus showed can never be repaid and should never be taken for granted. He died to remove all our sins by taking our deserved consequences upon Himself (1 John 3:5).He paid the price we would extract from ourselves, the debt others would demand from us, and the punishment the law required. The suffering He went through provided the miracle of forgiveness for us all (John 19:1–30).

Unfortunately, instead of embracing the gift of forgiveness, we often do the opposite by demonstrating we are in the right. We are unwilling to endure suffering for the sake of love, and we cling to our rules and accentuate the consequences of people's trespasses against us. To justify our unforgiveness and to achieve justice for the wrong that has been done, we depend on the enforcement of rules (naming sins with power to enforce compliance) and are motivated by self-preservation (a priority to protect one's safety, acceptance, and comfort). Jesus revealed this common practice to be an insufficient and sometimes dreadful solution. Treating one another poorly was supplanted by the way of forgiveness and love at the cross (Col. 2:13–15). Showing unconditional love, He willingly paid the price for everyone's sins to facilitate the restoration of relationships.

I find it extremely difficult to extend complete and sacrificial forgiveness without knowing the great forgiveness the cross demonstrates for us. Jesus' monumental embrace of our destruction was not only a demonstration of complete love and total forgiveness but also served to restore our relationship with God. We are restored to a relationship with a Father who loves us, holds us tight, never harms us, and wants what is best for His children. This relationship can be challenging to accept, knowing how much we have failed God, ourselves, and others. Our acceptance of His forgiveness and restoration to His family dramatically affects our ability to forgive others, even knowing all our earthly relationships can fall short and are subject to abuse.

Sometimes, our ability to forgive is held back by the pain of the past and the threat of future abuse. Forgiveness is especially difficult when it is tied to an intimate person in our lives—someone with whom we are vulnerable and who can hurt us repeatedly. Continued trespasses are exponentially destructive and can easily lead to bitterness and resentment. Can a wise and self-protecting person foolishly lend themselves to blind forgiveness to be abused by those who would hurt them?

The offense of adultery may be one of the most problematic cases of forgiveness to face because the consequences are so life-shattering. The betrayal can lead one's psyche to collapse emotionally and often has physical implications on the body. In the process of forgiveness, does the hurt party decide on a price to be extracted for the transgression? Does the offender extract payment from themselves? These responses are often insurmountable to overcome, yet in some cases, forgiveness can still bring reconciliation.

No matter how much we forgive, the consequences of the offenses do not disappear. We naturally want to flee or fight when we are personally hurt, which is the opposite of forgiveness and love leading to restoration. To forgive and stay in a relationship, we must adjust ourselves to bear the adverse outcomes of the transgression. It's not guaranteed, but God can salvage dreadful unintended consequences and weave them into a tapestry of the relationship. Although knowing this aspect helps, it does not make the restoration easier. Restoration is a decision to go against all instinctive reactions that demand self-protection—a decision to love despite the risk of loss to ourselves (Eph. 4:31–32).

Sadly, even with restoration, the paradise of vulnerability will never be the same. Things settle down, but each party will have trouble forgetting the betrayal. Trust has been broken, and nothing will change that. Life for the parties involved begins a new chapter in which they grow together and continue to learn to love and survive the scars. Restoring a healthy relationship after a willfully destructive betrayal of trust is no less than a miracle.

What makes the tension worse for the believer is that walking in God's love requires us to engage in constant and great forgiveness (Luke 17:4). Yet, the deeper we are hurt and impacted by sin, the harder it is to forgive and forget. Forgiveness does not change the reality that transgressions affect us and change us. Unfortunately, unforgiveness amplifies the impact by falsely guaranteeing our protection and awakening our vengeance––this is not the way of Christ.

Lack of forgiveness can be like an old, threadbare, dirty coat we carry for protection. Even though it has no benefit, we must keep it for when life gets too uncomfortable. Since it makes us feel safe, throwing it away is out of the question. This cloak of unforgiveness can significantly hinder us from experiencing the *good life* Jesus promises. It can represent our fear of abuse or hold our power to execute revenge. Refusal to forgive plays into our self-importance and produces resentment, judgment, and anger. If we feel someone is trying to hurt us, we can reach into a pocket and find past grievances to either block them or injure them first. Letting go is extremely hard. Unfortunately, keeping that old coat of unforgiveness perpetuates our hurt and loss, and holding on to our grievances is more detrimental to the bearer than it is to the objects of our wrath.

Enduring the destruction of another's trespass is a complex burden. This act of unconditional, sacrificial love includes a willingness to be vulnerable for the sake of love (Matt. 10:38–39). Love and vulnerability are a delicate balance—we must intently seek the guidance of the Spirit because we still need boundaries to survive. Boundaries are healthy and effective for protecting us and others, yet the Spirit can lead us to be dangerously vulnerable at times. God can grow our ability to be vulnerable as we learn more about His forgiveness and love. To reach the level of turning the other cheek, we must be steeped in God's love so deeply that we realize physical and emotional pain can be endured to demonstrate His love and forgiveness.

This idea of ridiculous vulnerability brings the fear of abuse. It is essential to know that forgiveness is different from reconciliation. While forgiving wrongs to have healthy, lasting relationships is often worth the risk, remaining in an abusive relationship can be tricky, even for a believer. In our strength, forgiveness and reconciliation may not seem possible. Perhaps somewhere between total self-protection and total sacrifice, we can facilitate forgiveness. Although a restored relationship may not be on the table, there still can be forgiveness and letting go of hostilities.

In the worst of circumstances, only His sacrificial and unconditional love—the type of love found at the cross—could be powerful enough to motivate us to take on the magnitude of the destruction caused by the offending person to have a relationship with them. Forgiveness is messy, no matter the transgression. All our actions have consequences, and it is a mistake to think forgiveness is a way to rid ourselves of them. Instead, it is a way to love amid the consequences. Forgiveness is a way in, not a way out.

Jesus is our model and motivation to forgive others. The forgiveness of the cross transformed the world, demonstrating forgiveness through sacrificial love. If we let Him, the Holy Spirit can work the miracle of forgiveness in our hearts and minds. It's a process of the Spirit moving us to forgive, forget, and restore relationships with others—and He moves us to forgive ourselves. We walk in His grace, knowing that God has completely erased all our sins and that we will not be judged for our failures (Ps. 103:12,

John 5:24). This gives us freedom from our past and an assurance that we can let go and move on, free from our failures and their eternal consequences. The more we understand and receive God's complete forgiveness, as the Spirit transforms us, the more we are empowered to experience and share this great gift. Forgiveness may seem easy to call for, yet it is an immensely difficult act of sacrificial love done in the power of the Spirit after receiving our complete forgiveness from Jesus first.

The goal of God's love and grace on the cross was not merely to remove our debts but also to make us loving and forgiving people. God's forgiveness is demonstrated in our lives when the Holy Spirit's indwelling and the Son's love and forgiveness work hand in hand to transform us into a new creation. As I humbly live in God's unconditional love and forgiveness, while filled with His Spirit, I hope I am compelled to extend the same love and forgiveness to others. In practice, as we receive more love from the Spirit, we become more willing and able to love and forgive beyond our natural ability.

PART 3: ARRIVING AT A GOOD LIFE

Chapter 20: A Good Life for the Least of These

And these three remain: faith, hope, and love. But the greatest of these is love.

First Corinthians 13:13 (NET)

I HOPE HEARING THE story of life and death for a troubled man named Kraig will benefit your understanding of how the *good life* can come to the least expected. Even though he was a disabled, middle-aged man who had just been paroled from prison for auto theft and drug charges, I still found myself fortunate to meet this child of God.

I enjoyed knowing Kraig in his last couple of years. He attended a Bible study I led at a local bar in the neighborhood. At that time, Kraig had an abundance of health problems, lingering trouble with the legal system, and still dabbled with drugs. He would attend consistently for a while and then suddenly stop coming. Kraig cycled between pulling himself out of a hole and falling back into the same pit.

During one of his downturns, I visited him in the hospital. At that time, I could see a glimpse of Kraig's relationship with God and his family. He spoke of his love for his son and that he wished he could have done more for him. He told me about his stepdaughters and how he cared for them and tried to be a part of their lives. Most of all, Kraig loved his mom and dad and appreciated all they had done for him, believing in his potential despite his troubles. He wanted to help them in return when he got well.

I vividly remember how much Kraig's mom and dad loved him. Their love will always inspire me and remind me of God's love. When they adopted Kraig as an infant, they committed to loving him and never stopped. They never gave up on him, even when he made it extremely difficult.

Kraig was amazingly resilient despite all his trials and still had a great time with those around him. He always tried to remain hopeful for what was coming next, yet most of the possible paths in his life had somewhat bleak outcomes and seemed to telegraph struggle and despair.

The following passage is an excerpt from the sermon I wrote for his funeral:

> We all struggle. We all are sinners. We all make mistakes. The question is: "Do you know what Kraig knew?" Jesus paid the price for his mistakes. Kraig knew who Jesus was and what Jesus did for him. Since Kraig knew Jesus, he was no longer a sinner but a saint. Jesus made him clean; in the same way, He can make all of us clean.

The disciple Matthew wrote of Jesus' encounter with a leper:

> After he came down from the mountain, large crowds followed him. And a leper approached, and bowed low before him, saying, "Lord, if you are willing, you can make me clean." He stretched out his hand and touched him saying, "I am willing. Be clean!" Immediately his leprosy was cleansed.
>
> Matthew 8:1–3 (NET)

Lepers were so unclean that no one would dare to touch them. They were required to do the ancient equivalent of wearing a mask and social distancing. The Jewish culture of the day considered them not only cursed with sickness but also cursed with an evil, sinful life as well. They were outcasts from society and left to die. Jesus reached down and touched the outcast and made him clean. The man went from sinner to saint with one touch.

Kraig told me he knew Jesus had saved him but that he still failed continually and made mistakes. I believe, if he had a chance to do things over, he would have chosen a different path. At one point, I encouraged Kraig to try to see how God could use him to bless others based on the experiences he had overcome. This was a challenging prospect for him because it meant he still had to conquer some of his bad habits, which he felt he could not do.

Despite all his failures, he continued to grow as a believer until his last day. Weeks before his death, he worked hard to complete a five-book Bible study series, which gave his family great comfort in knowing the sincerity of his faith.

John quotes Jesus as saying:

Very truly I tell you, whoever hears my word and believes him who sent me has eternal life and will not be judged but has crossed over from death to life.

> John 5:24 (NIV)

We know that Kraig physically passed from life to death on August 1st. We also know that on the day he believed in Jesus, he passed from death to life. He had eternal life in him at that very moment, long before he fell asleep for the last time. Kraig did not have to wait until his passing to be with Jesus, nor do we. Jesus enters us and gives us eternal life as soon as we believe. The spiritual person we knew as Kraig didn't actually die; he merely changed rooms. He's no longer sitting around in our living room—he's in God's home now, sitting in the presence of Jesus. Someday, I, too, will be in God's house relaxing with Kraig.

Kraig was not, and will not, be judged for his wrongs because he is forgiven according to Christ's work on the cross. Christ took away all his sins and smiled at all his goodness. Kraig believed in Jesus, and it was credited to him as righteousness.

As you see all the wonderful pictures of Kraig on the screen, you realize how blessed his life was, except for a few bad decisions. That is the same for all of us. We're not any better as far as failure goes. We all have a few bad decisions hidden in our lives. Believing in Jesus, as Kraig did, changes us from sinners to saints despite our transgressions. All who have received the forgiveness and eternal life that Jesus gives will someday rejoin Kraig in God's living room as we hang out with Jesus.

Knowing Kraig's circumstances, it appears he struggled to find a *good life*. Yet as we contemplate Kraig's salvation, we learn that he was a new creation in Christ, as equally loved by Jesus as you and I. His story exemplifies one of the main driving forces that led me to question whether our new abundant life is found in the traditional ideas about sanctification. If I were ever to go back to believing in sanctification by works, I would have trouble explaining where that leaves Kraig and where that leaves me in terms of our sanctification. I would also wonder if there was something I could do that would keep me from heaven. Where does that leave all the great Christian men and women who served God with their lives yet fell drastically and committed grave evils? Where does that leave the thief on the cross?

There will always be people who say they cannot let go of rules and cannot take what I am saying about the end of the law to be correct. I sat with a seminary student who was twenty years younger than me to discuss Christianity. He was more intelligent than I am, and his biblical and theological studies were fresh on his mind. He discussed with me his grand plans to write a book about the fall in Genesis and I spoke of my understanding of sanctification. Sadly, we talked past each other for four long hours. In the fifth hour, I began to listen and understand what he was saying, and he, too, began to comprehend the ideas I was presenting. He disagreed with how I presented sanctification, but he looked directly at me and made this enlightening statement: "I really want what you're saying to be true, but I don't believe it is."

I hope you, as a dedicated reader, are close to understanding what I am writing after reading this far in the book. I am trying to share with you what I said to the young seminarian: "It is true! God is that good, and He loves us so much that He died to set us free from sin and the law." If you can get a glimpse of the freedom He has given us to live a life of truth and love in a Spirit-led relationship with Him, then my writing and your reading this book have all been worth it, and I believe a *good life* with Jesus is in your future.

At this point in the book, it would be nice if I could summarize all I have written into easy instructions on how to live this *good life* I am touting. I wish that were possible. Even if we had the perfect plan and detailed instructions regarding what to do with every variable, there would be no guarantees, and we know from experience that we would likely fail at carrying it out. Therefore, the insights I have communicated come with a caveat: this world is broken, and we are far from perfect. Sadly, as we travel through this life, tragedy strikes as often as triumph. For many, life can feel like a mundane, non-eventful existence. Even worse, a significant number of humans will never even get a chance to merely take a breath. Consequently, any idea I have given you about finding His *good life* must come with the understanding that it will help as much as it applies to your life.

Gratefully, many of us are given long lives without harrowing hardships. Life brings many ups and downs, and with each turn we will enjoy varying degrees of understanding as to how God's salvific truth applies. The Spirit takes each Christian on their own personal journey. Jesus moves us closer to His truth and love through the power of the Holy Spirit. Some start far away and only progress a little, while others seem to touch heaven. Life is not the same for everyone; it is not equal nor what we could call fair. We have missed the point if we see this journey as arriving somewhere. It is a process of daily walking by our faith in Jesus, knowing the truth of our salvation, which gives us hope for the future, and exhibiting as much heavenly love as possible.

Knowing that everyone's life is unique does not negate the idea that we can seek to find a common thread that enables us to participate in the *good life* Jesus promised. That common thread is found in the knowing the basics of salvation. First, eternal life is given immediately upon placing our faith in Jesus. Once we believe in Jesus as God and decide to follow Him, we become God's children and He gives us the Holy Spirit as a down payment for eternal life (2 Cor. 1:22, John 5:24). Second, we must know that Jesus loved us so much that He died to take away our sins (John 1:29), which frees us from sin and law and removes all condemnation and threat of separation from God

(Rom. 8:1–2, 8:38-39). Third, we must understand and believe the truth that God loves us and wants what is best for us (1 John 3:1–2). This gives us hope that can carry us through the trials we will face as believers. These three principles are foundational to begin our journey with the Spirit towards the *good life*.

It is imperative to know that the *good life* we seek is not found in worldly blessings of riches, glory, or comfort but in a spiritual existence that goes way beyond temporal pleasures. It is found by seeking the spiritual blessings that come through an intimate relationship with God and understanding that earthly blessings come through His Spirit teaching us to love others as Jesus loves us. Living life by these truths of our salvation, in the power of the Spirit, sets us free to experience a new, *good life* in Christ, dominated by love and free from sin.

Love is the most important gift the Spirit pours into our hearts. Without love, a meaningful life is challenging to realize. Love informs us that others are as important as ourselves and are worthy of our sacrifice. What is the purpose of experiencing life if we have no one to share it with? Love instructs us to give and not take. Love mandates us to listen and tell the truth. Love is the deep, moving action and emotion that powers our lives towards goodness and greatness. On the flip side, without it, our lights go out.

I have written about how life can be dark at different times, but knowing the truth, which brings the gift of our salvation, allows hope to spring to life in our darkness. We should not live in the possibilities of despair; we must reside in the hope of a great ending. Even in the darkest times, seeing the hope of our future with Jesus makes it brighter.

It is incredible and inspirational to look into the eyes of a beautiful soul who still has their hope in Jesus, even when they know their days are numbered because they are dying of cancer. I was privileged to meet an inspiring woman at a youth event who was very interested in who I was and had so much love in her eyes. I glanced down at her hands covered in a light cloth bandage, and her bones were visible at the ends of her fingers where they stuck out through her wrappings. It was at that moment I knew she was dying. I was touched that a person, days from death, could be so generous and loving. Knowing the truth of her salvation caused the hope for her future to burn brightly in her.

Most of us are not facing such an immediate tragedy, but we still have our own dark battles with adverse circumstances in our lives. We can cultivate hope by trusting in the best possible outcome with the Spirit comforting us, not by dwelling on the worst scenario we can conjure up in our minds. We have a choice to live with hope for the best, knowing that our Father is in control, or we can live without the certainty of this truth, and live in the fear of the unknown. Life has bad days, but the truth is our heavenly Father has a good plan for our future, which lets us know that bad days do not have to win.

In addition to the gifts of love and hope, we must not forget the gift of faith. I often contemplate the darkness of thinking this short life is all there is. What would we have if we had no God, no afterlife, no self beyond the chemicals and electrical signals, and existed merely as a structure of flesh and bones? I have believed in God my whole life, except for flirting with the idea of abandoning Him when I was fourteen, so it is difficult for me to conceive of a world where He does not exist. If this short existence is all there is, faith goes away, and hope fades with its passing. I would be left with little reason to live a life of kindness and productivity without my faith in a creator who loves me.

The faith that I am professing begins with the belief in the idea of a loving creator God who is in control and was proven true in the person of Jesus. When God walked the earth, it went beyond the general reality of a God and proposed a personal God who loves us and desires to know us. Jesus, God incarnate, was sent by the Father to sacrifice Himself to have this relationship. The Father resurrected Jesus from the dead, demonstrating great hope by displaying His power over death and His ability to orchestrate everything according to His perfect plan. The Father calls us to be His children, and He promises to send the Spirit to walk with us in our struggles and celebrate with us in our successes. He loves us as a parent who never compromises their love for their child. Our believing these truths about Him is the faith that He wants us to have.

Finding the elusive *good life* and keeping it when we find it are challenging quests. The Spirit bolsters our faith in the supernatural, increases our hope in resolving our troubles, and guides us to exhibit unconditional, sacrificial love as Jesus did. The closer we are to perfecting His faith, hope, and love in us, the closer we are to the promised *good life*, a life turned *love-side-up*.

Chapter 21: Why Does a Good Life Include Suffering?

For I consider that our present sufferings cannot even be compared to the glory that will be revealed to us.

Romans 8:18 (NET)

WHEN WE COME TO CHRIST, He does not make our lives perfect. Christians suffer from all the same problems as those who do not follow Jesus. We still lose our spouses and face times when friends and family no longer love us. We are not immune to persecution, being accused of crimes, or losing all our money due to theft or our own mishaps. Our loved ones can and will die, and even our young children might suffer from disease or injury. The experiences of humanity's common sufferings are universal for everyone, with or without Christ.

Christians are also not exempt from social problems and mental health issues. The need for affirmation still dominates our interactions and we fail to love daily. We can lack a sense of purpose, well-being, joy, and peace. We have the same difficulties deciding on a career and finding a companion to spend our lives with. We are equally likely to live with despair, angst, and boredom. Inner problems can still plague us, and we may even need psychological help with our broken minds. As a Christian, we certainly do not avoid the imperative to forgive others and ourselves. We continue to share in humanity's struggle to be well adjusted, to be in relationship and do something meaningful with our lives.

I remember going to a Billy Graham crusade and being in awe of how he convinced us that God cares about our struggles and problems. He communicated that surrendering our lives to Jesus could improve our messy existence. Oh how right he was, but each of us woke up the next morning in the same predicament we had been in the night before. Our hearts had changed but little had changed in our actual lives. Jesus is the foundational answer we need to cope with suffering, yet one crusade does not bring about the lasting, life-changing transformation we need. It's the process God does in our hearts, before and after the crusade that brings the change, subduing the evil and suffering in our lives, and if given time, the world around us.

Knowing that it is a process and not a one-time event, gives us some insight into how we can persevere and survive our suffering—great or small—and continue to hold to our belief in the idea of a good God who doesn't fail us. Even with personal hardships in our lives, we can continue to believe in a loving God who works out all things for the good (Rom. 8:28).

We know God is good, even though in His infinite wisdom He allows evil to exist. When God gave humanity free will, it necessitated humans' ability to do evil. Consequently, as a result of the fall, evil and suffering came into the world.

To keep free will, God cannot step in and instantly cure all evil. Although the destruction experienced when evil occurs is very disheartening, if God worked a miracle in every case, He would impose the supernatural on our free will in such a way that we would have no choice but to believe in Him. This answer is not comforting when we are on the receiving end of a disaster or a disease, yet we must experience the natural in a way that leaves us to wonder if the supernatural is real—otherwise, the indisputable knowledge of God would limit our free will.

When we face suffering, it is too easy to reject God's control and believe we humans can somehow save ourselves, while at the same time, we ironically live in fear of everything spiraling out of control. When in control, too often, ruling humans seem to think safety is reached by micromanaging the lives of others to achieve their desired results. This can create even worse suffering and limit humanity's freedom. For instance, if driving were eliminated, there would be no deaths by car wrecks, but the lack of production would send the world into a tailspin. Living a full and free life, trusting in God's providence, even though there are disasters, is far superior to living a life restricted by fear with the questionable notion of safety from disaster. Knowing God's control gives us appropriate freedom to live vibrantly in a world full of pitfalls, even though it is a dangerous freedom.

When people rebel against God in their freedom and begin to abuse their fellow humans, they face His divine judgment. He sometimes allows or even orchestrates circumstances many would consider evil. In the past, He has not restrained a natural disaster or sent human-orchestrated destruction to fall upon people who have ceased to love their fellow humans properly. God has allowed what we call evil to facilitate justice as a necessary step in restraining a worse evil, which may have occurred if He had not stepped in. This idea is demonstrated in the Old Testament as God rebukes the nations, including Israel, for their sins. Sometimes, when allowed to suffer the horrific consequences of their actions, humanity can recognize their error and make a correction.

While some may feel that God allowing evil and suffering, or even causing it, precludes Him from being thought of as good, the Bible displays a different picture. Scripture shows God's overwhelming love for mankind and His committed pursuit of a personal relationship with us. Although God desires to help us in our suffering, He knows we need to reach a point at which we will accept a Savior and give up trying to fix ourselves on our own—and maybe will even stop trying to build our kingdom without Him.

The Father did something way beyond correcting and warning us. He sent Jesus as a substitutionary payment to save us from our sin and rebellion and to restore our relationship with Him. Even though reconciliation with God does not end our suffering, it restores meaning and purpose in the struggles we face. Our Savior's example shows us that learning to love in the midst of suffering is more important than fixing or preventing it.

Even with the understanding of the purpose and inevitability of suffering, we may still wonder why Jesus doesn't step in and at least take care of our ailments as He did in New Testament times. Physical healing seems a just reward for those who choose to follow Him, yet it is often not the miracle God decides to do. Christ warned us that we would have trouble: "I have told you these things, so that in me you may have peace. In this world you will have trouble. But take heart! I have overcome the world" (John

16:33, NIV). He also said, "Take my yoke upon you and learn from me, for I am gentle and humble in heart, and you will find rest for your souls. For my yoke is easy and my burden is light." (Matt. 11:29–30, NIV). Jesus seemed to clearly understand the human condition of suffering and struggle, but instead of removing difficulty from our lives, on the cross He demonstrated the idea of embracing trials for the sake of love.

When we follow Jesus, instead of automatically healing us and taking away our physical suffering, God's primary concern is to bless us with the Holy Spirit and to change our hearts from death to life. This transformation is far greater than physical healing and lasts for an eternity. God delivers us from the deceptions of thinking everything is about appeasing the flesh, to a life of love and truth achieved by walking in the Spirit. God creates this miraculous transformation of change by Jesus abiding in us through the Spirit, and by us sincerely seeking Him with our spirit, heart, mind and strength. This is the change we need most, not deliverance from suffering. We are confident He will not fail to move us toward a life of love, and toward a life of peace and joy as we walk with Jesus as our king.

God can and does choose to heal us physically, on occasion, but this healing is usually temporary because none of us get out of this world alive. Our bodies die as a result of Adam's curse on the world, and life can also be shortened by some of our own choices and the actions of others. In salvation, when we understand we are no longer cursed, the physical seems less important, even when wracked with pain and suffering. Knowing that our love for Jesus and others can grow amid our suffering frees and challenges us. If God eliminated all our struggles, is it possible we would cease to grow in love for others? It is a mystery why God chooses to heal in some cases and not others. Again, we are left to have faith that God is in control and that His sovereign plan will work out in the end.

I am not saying that God does not heal us from physical ailments, for I have personal experience that He does. In 2011, when Jesus healed my clotting disease, roughly about a year after my hospital stay with two blood clots in my lungs, He impressed a verse upon my conscience: "My grace is sufficient for you, for My strength is made perfect in weakness" (2 Cor. 12:9, NKJV). I truly felt Jesus saying to me, "I will heal you of clotting, but I am leaving you with symptoms of pain in your muscles so you will be weak and humble and learn that I am the source of your strength." That is precisely what happened. One year after being diagnosed, my clotting factor was reversed—a one-in-a-million chance, according to my doctor. My muscle pain remained as God had impressed on me it would. Both the healing and the pain were gifts from God.

I could not disagree with God on the gift of pain. I knew I could not slow down; there was too much to do. I believed I could do almost any task with strength, intelligence, and determination. Instead of doing all the complicated tasks at work, I needed to slow down and teach others. I needed to slow down at home, value my family, and spend time with them. Intellectually, I was inspired to stop depending on my past learning, dive deep into God's Word, and learn the depths of His love.

Still, I have fallen short of His calling to love in my weakness. It also seems my coworkers, my family, my friends, my brain, and my attitudes are not always willing participants in God's calling to depend on Him for strength.

I don't see my health struggles as negative events in my life because they have resulted in my spiritual growth. As I approach my struggles, I understand they are a necessary part of life to teach me to love, be humble, and sacrifice. I feel well-taught to depend on Him.

Strangely, suffering can lead to healthy growth for some, and for others, it can lead to bitterness and possibly evil. As believers, how we respond to suffering is part of God's eternal growth process. Struggle raises the question: Can we see God's work in our lives despite all the suffering? This question may be challenging to answer, even if "we know that all things work together for good for those who love God, who are called according to his purpose" (Rom. 8:28, NET). To embrace our suffering, it is necessary to understand that through struggle, He conforms us to "the image of His Son" so that we might be glorified by having the opportunity to demonstrate the same love He showed us (Rom. 8:29–30, NET).

Hopefully, we will understand that struggle, and sometimes even suffering, are tools God uses to teach us His truths and expand our ability to love. Without any struggle, we might be tempted to disregard God, our friends, and possibly even our family if it means a better life for ourselves. Hardships force us to evaluate and choose what is essential. When we have it too easy, we may fall prey to differentiating ourselves from others and judging those around us as lesser because our circumstances seem superficially better. A person who avoids struggle might lack empathy and compassion for others.

Paul goes so far as to say our struggle is good and not to be feared or regretted. Paul wrote in his letter to the Romans about how Jesus redeemed suffering:

> Therefore, since we have been declared righteous by faith, we have peace with God through our Lord Jesus Christ, through whom we have also obtained access by faith into this grace in which we stand, and we rejoice in the hope of God's glory. Not only this, but we also rejoice in sufferings, knowing that suffering produces endurance, and endurance, character, and character, hope. And hope does not disappoint, because the love of God has been poured out in our hearts through the Holy Spirit who was given to us.
>
> Romans 5:1–5 (NET)

What an incredible miracle when Jesus uses suffering to change the bad part of who we are, replacing it with endurance, character, and hope.

By faith, God gives us hope. He begins to modify the behaviors that contribute to our suffering, which empowers us to change. It is almost like we are juxtaposing guilt, shame, depression, greed, anger, slander, violence, perversion, and manipulation with Jesus' offer of salvation and regeneration, in which God supplies our needs for love, kindness, peace, contentment, compassion, and concern. God begins our restoration during our suffering. He begins fulfilling our needs through His presence in us and healing our emotional and mental suffering. He directs us to build ourselves up instead of tearing ourselves down. He teaches us to give to others instead of taking from them. He produces ever-increasing endurance and character, bolstered with love because God pours out His love in our hearts through His Spirit. His ever-increasing love demonstrates our transformation through suffering. As we live by the Spirit in His love, the worst circumstances cannot destroy our inner self which is in relationship with God. Instead of destruction, we experience growth by being taught to love and hope during our suffering.

A Christian may put too little emphasis on embracing what God does through struggle. Instead, they may put too much emphasis on avoiding struggle and gaining success by worldly standards through building their kingdom—or what they think is God's kingdom. His kingdom is not happiness according to worldly standards. Jesus came to bring personal peace, but our commitment to Him may also bring strife with others and even strife with ourselves as we grow (Luke 14:26). Jesus also said we must take up our cross (carry our beam of suffering) and follow Him if we want to be His disciples (Luke 14:27). He proclaimed, "Whoever desires to save his life will lose it, but whoever loses his life for My sake will save it" (Luke 9:24, NKJV). It is essential to not see struggles as punishment from God; instead, struggles should be seen as growing experiences to be lived and loved through—or at least survived—with God's love and grace. Struggles are God's tool in this fallen world to grow us to eternity (Rom. 5:1–5).

In addition, since we are called to be willing to suffer for the sake of spreading His good news of the possibility of a loving relationship with God through Jesus, we must not shrink from our trials (Jas 1:2-4). Jesus is our greatest inspiration, given He suffered to reconcile us to Himself when we did not deserve it. Because of His great sacrifice, we can boldly endure suffering, if necessary, to communicate the gospel of reconciliation with God.

As we face our struggles with His Spirit in us and the grace, love, truth, and hope He brings, we grow eternally in our souls. We become more like God intends us to be for eternity. We begin to participate in our eternal life immediately as we grow in His love. The apostle Paul once more pontificates on suffering in chapter eight of his letter to the Romans:

> And if children, then heirs (namely, heirs of God and also fellow heirs with Christ)—if indeed we suffer with him so we may also be glorified with him. For I consider that our present sufferings cannot even be compared to the glory that will be revealed to us. For the creation eagerly waits for the revelation of the sons of God. For the creation was subjected to futility [violence]—not

willingly but because of God who subjected it—in hope that the creation itself will also be set free from the bondage of decay into the glorious freedom of God's children. For we know that the whole creation groans and suffers together until now. Not only this, but we ourselves also, who have the first fruits of the Spirit, groan inwardly as we eagerly await our adoption, the redemption of our bodies.

Romans 8:17–23 (NET)

Our world's violence brings suffering to each person and creation as well. We all, including creation, wait for an end to the reign of evil and suffering when love reigns again and our bodies are redeemed.

As we endure suffering and struggle, it no longer produces death in us but now produces eternal life. With God's Spirit of truth and love indwelling us, we can embrace life without fear of loss or strife because it is all a part of God's creation and His plan. We no longer need to manage our lives to alleviate or avoid suffering; we manage this life with the compass of His Spirit, teaching us to love. We seek a new life of ultimate experience that God gives us as we grow towards our eternal selves while facing hardships. Suffering is not our enemy, nor should we hate the people who cause it. Christ redeemed suffering and now uses it for His glory. He commanded us to follow His example of being willing to suffer to demonstrate His love, in the hope of reconciling people to God.

James wrote that we are to think of suffering and struggle as good because all of our new lives are under the direction of God (Jas 1:2). Both the hugs and the punches are elements of the new life Jesus gives us. Renewed by the Spirit and bathed in His love, we are worthy to receive the hugs and have the strength to endure the punches; responding to both appropriately can bring praise to God and grow eternal life in us. This, in effect, is perfecting the love of the cross in our lives and it will turn our world *love-side-up*.

Chapter 22: Love Is the Key

We have come to know love by this: that Jesus laid down his life for us; thus we ought to lay down our lives for our fellow Christians.

First John 3:16 (NET)

HOW DOES ONE DEFINE love? Our hearts are moved at the mention of heroic acts of love—a person donating a kidney to save a friend or a soldier diving on a grenade to protect their comrades. Fictional stories of love in movies and books emotionally draw us in. The personal experience of losing someone we love devastates us. We smile when we see someone speak to a child in an uplifting way that changes the child's whole demeanor or even their life.

To define love, the quintessential place to look is the cross. Although we know this is the ultimate demonstration of love, we often struggle to understand how sacrificial love is applied on a practical, day-to-day basis. Opportunities for grand heroism are rare, but giving hugs, doing dishes, saying kind words, and working hard to make ends meet may be the acts of love Jesus leads us to. As we follow the Spirit, expressions of God's love look a little different for each of us.

A traditional way to define love is to consult the Oxford English Dictionary. Here, we find a profound definition of religious love:

> [Love is] the benevolence and affection of God towards an individual or towards creation; (also) the affectionate devotion due to God from an individual; regard and consideration of one

human being towards another prompted by a sense of a common relationship to God.[32]

This is a beautiful description of the love a believer should have for God and others. The definition also clearly depicts the source of our ability to love as coming from God, which is a profoundly religious statement coming from an irreligious book.

Here are two interesting and pertinent musings on love: one by the great Dostoyevsky and the other by the thought-provoking Kurt Vonnegut.

> What is hell? I maintain that it is the suffering of being unable to love.
>
> Fyodor Dostoyevsky, *The Brothers Karamazov*[33]

> A purpose of human life, no matter who is controlling it, is to love whoever is around to be loved.
>
> Kurt Vonnegut, *The Sirens of Titan*[34]

The authors agree on the importance of love to life, even though they come from very different backgrounds and lived a lifetime apart.

Often, when people talk of love, they speak in terms of its application, its presence, and its absence. Love is a quality of one's behavior we know is either there or missing, but we find it difficult to quantify. Yet, love is not simply an uncontrollable force; it includes a voluntary decision to act.

If I were to attempt to narrow down a definition of love, I would say that human love toward another incorporates a desire to know and value a person as they are, combined with a deep desire to do what is best for them and a sincere willingness to sacrifice to give them what they need—even at one's great loss. This definition of love is made possible by unconditional acceptance based on our willingness to embrace others as they are and set aside our urge to make them what we want them to be. Selfless love can only be achieved through the Spirit as He enables us to genuinely consider others more important than ourselves, and as He gives us the ability to not hold the wrongs of others against them. Loving by the power of the Spirit ultimately transforms us to see the world with an attitude of *what I can give* not *what I can get*—which is the core aspect of true love (Phil. 2:3–5; 1 Cor. 13; Rom. 5:6–8).

Greg Boyd, Ph.D., pastor of Woodland Hills Church in Saint Paul, Minnesota, and former professor at Bethel University, gives a similar definition of cross-type love in his 2013 sermon entitled "Sociopath Religion,"

> Enemy embracing, other-oriented, self-sacrificial, non-violent love ...ascribe[s] unsurpassable and unconditional worth to every other human being on the planet ...instead of sacrificing them, we sacrifice ourselves for them. ...The world is not capable of [this type of love]. To get this kind of love ...surrendering your life to Abba Father and letting him download his character into your life—it's called the Holy Spirit. ...We can't crank this one out on our own; our self-preservationist instincts ...are too strong to will our way into this.[35]

Boyd describes love in an intense, powerful, challenging, and inspiring way. He argues this love will only come to fruition through the power of the Holy Spirit.

Almost two thousand years ago, the apostle Paul wrote the quintessential, authoritative, and informative treatise on love. Paul described the gift of love as the "way that is beyond comparison" (1 Cor. 12:31, NET). It is an other-worldly description:

> If I speak in the tongues of men or of angels, but do not have love, I am only a resounding gong or a clanging cymbal. If I have the gift of prophecy and can fathom all mysteries and all knowledge, and if I have a faith that can move mountains but do not have love, I am nothing. If I give all I possess to the poor and give over my body to hardship that I may boast, but do not have love, I gain nothing. Love is patient, love is kind. It does not envy, it does not boast, it is not proud. It does not dishonor others, it is not

self-seeking, it is not easily angered, it keeps no record of wrongs. Love does not delight in evil but rejoices with the truth. It always protects, always trusts, always hopes, always perseveres. Love never fails. But where there are prophecies, they will cease; where there are tongues, they will be stilled; where there is knowledge, it will pass away. For we know in part and we prophesy in part, but when completeness comes, what is in part disappears. When I was a child, I talked like a child, I thought like a child, I reasoned like a child. When I became a man, I put the ways of childhood behind me. For now we see only a reflection as in a mirror; then we shall see face to face. Now I know in part; then I shall know fully, even as I am fully known. And now these three remain: faith, hope and love. But the greatest of these is love.

First Corinthians 13:1–13 (NIV)

In this extraordinary statement, Paul explains the necessity of love, what love is and is not, the primacy of love, the clarity of love, the maturity of love, and the eternality of love. When one sits and tries to define or explain love, they quickly discover how extraordinary this passage is in portraying genuine love.

Even with a good definition and well-worded instructions, love can be exceedingly difficult to demonstrate in our day-to-day lives. The desire for possessions, personal affirmation, and physical attention distract us. We want to be heard, to be important, to be safe—and sometimes, we want to feel we are better than our neighbors. We can be driven to have correct politics, a respectable spiritual direction, and an admirable morality. Judgment of ourselves and others overwhelms us. In our own strength, we can fail to love, especially if we use reasoned arguments and religious morals to prop ourselves up. We may defend our unloving actions by appealing to experts and hiding behind our emotions. We also may blame circumstances and others for our lack of love instead of recognizing our foolish, selfish behavior. Our pride and unwillingness to be humble can block the possibility of change in our lives. To become a loving person is no easy task: "There is no one righteous, not even one" (Rom. 3:10, NIV).

Love is a decision that can be driven by our emotions, reasoned by our minds, and, for Christians, empowered by the Spirit—often all at the same time. We may find ourselves entangled in our attempts to be loved and to give love. Sometimes, we're unsure how to respond when we receive loving acts of kindness. Someone may give us a hand when we are down, buy us a meal for no apparent reason, or kindly overlook our inappropriate behavior—and love us anyway.

Early experiences of love, namely from our parents or caregivers, are essential to our ability to love others. Our first encounter with love should be from our mothers. They give and model this wonderful gift when they provide their children with kind service and attention. Children who were not nurtured by their mothers are sometimes unable to recover from this deficit, no matter how much love is shown to them later in life. Even when the mother is a fallen person who cannot love them, people will spend a lifetime pursuing their mother's love that they missed. A father's love also has an invaluable impact, and it often comes in the form of gentle but firm teaching, correction, and encouraging words. When done right, the father displays an example of strength with tenderness that the child needs. Children without a mother and father's love will struggle to give and receive love, especially if no caregiver is there to make up the deficit.

Raising a child isn't easy. Caregivers must balance their wills and desires with their obligations. They deal with careers, personal brokenness, failure, success, disillusionment, pride, and—at times—physical ailments, including mental struggles. They may need to overcome tremendous hurdles to be able to demonstrate their love. Perhaps the difficulties they transcend are what make their loving acts so meaningful. We desire someone to make a great sacrifice for us because it communicates and affirms our value. For many, that sacrificial person may have been a parent, relative, or a caring friend; for all, that person is Jesus.

In our discussion and attempt to understand love, we must never lose our focus on Jesus as our example and source of love. Jesus exhibited the greatest love ever known when He, the creator of the universe, volunteered to die on the cross to save us from our sins and reconcile us to Himself. He died in our place, setting us free from our brokenness, gifting us to know a loving God, and empowering us to love others. On the cross, Jesus demonstrated sacrificial love as a new way to live in contrast to a violent, self-serving humanity. He did not come to fix the world according to human definitions of right and wrong; Jesus came to make our relationship right with Him, right with others, and right with ourselves. He came to teach us to love and to give us the ability to love.

Jesus didn't just demonstrate His love on the cross. With the shedding of His blood, He established a new covenant relationship with only two duties: to believe in Him and His work on the cross, and to "love one another." (John 13:34, NET). He turned our lives *love-side-up* with His new command to live with the sacrificial love of the cross.

As disciples of Jesus, we are to follow the way of love, which transforms how we interact with the law. Paul clarified this by writing: "Love does no harm to a neighbor. Therefore, love is the fulfillment of the law" (Rom. 13:10, NIV). The insight that "love is the fulfillment of the law" is not an instruction to follow the law in order to love. It is the wrong conclusion to surmise from this verse that the law teaches us how to love our neighbor, and therefore, to know how to love, one should follow the law and the prophets. While love may fulfill the requirements of the law, following the law does not satisfy the requirements of love. The new commandment is not to go back to living by the law to learn to love. Not at all. Instead, if we love as Jesus loves, we will inevitably fulfill the law—and much more. The new covenant, with its only stipulation being to love, replaced the covenant of the Mosaic law, which Jesus completed and nailed to the cross (Col. 2:14). Having the love of Jesus as our new commandment and completely letting go of the old law to be good frees us to live and love by the Spirit, which begins our experience of the *good life* by turning our world *love-side-up*.

The Apostle John restates this command to love as the readiness "to lay down our lives for our fellow Christians" (1 John 3:16, NET). This sacrificial attitude does not come by following our knowledge of what we think is good and evil. The willingness to love and sacrifice for others comes from the Spirit and flows out of our relationship with Jesus. While all human beings are capable of acts of love, it is different for the believer. The Spirit offers inspiration and empowerment to continually love beyond our human abilities and without expectation of return. Jesus' example, and the Spirit's guidance drive us to look past all the roadblocks others put up and choose to act in a way that benefits them anyway, even if the personal cost is high.

This new way of sanctification, based on loving as Jesus loved, is in sharp contrast to being righteous through following moral laws or human virtues to be good. The *love-side-up* way of the cross proclaims that following rules does not make us good and, therefore, more loving; living in His love is what sanctifies us and makes us good. Reducing suffering does not make us more loving; loving with God's love reduces suffering. Working on the "fruits of the Spirit" in our lives does not make us more virtuous; living by the Spirit grows the "fruits of the Spirit" in us, especially love (Gal. 5:18, 22–23). Exalting virtues over and above submission to the supremacy of the sacrificial love of the cross and the Spirit's work can produce a proud person who appears to be morally righteous on the outside but does not have a love of the cross on the inside.

Being guided by the Spirit to live by love is the process of sanctification that no law can come close to motivating us to do. While the law gave us guidelines of what was not love, it was powerless to direct us to make loving choices on a relational basis, where love is needed most (Rom. 8:3). How do we respond when a family member is angry at us or when someone needs our last twenty dollars? We need to know the right words to say and the right actions to take in the moment––especially when to share our time with our spouse and kids, to communicate to them how valuable they are. Eliminating sin according to the law is no longer our focus or the problem; being perfected in God's love is now the path we follow.

Seeking to allow God to change us in His love is how we become more like what we will be in eternity. Eternal life is not just in the future—it is the gift God has bestowed on us right here in the present. He has given us "the Spirit in our hearts as a down payment" (2 Cor. 1:22, NET). Our eternal selves begin at our salvation. When we love God and love one another, as we walk with the Spirit through the easy and the trying circumstances we find ourselves in, we experience His new life in us. The more we realize His presence and share His unconditional love, the more we will experience the eternal transformation the Spirit accomplishes in our lives.

How far does this call to love go? Should we be like Mother Teresa, who gave her whole life to serve and love the dying in Calcutta? She sacrificed the world's enticements which enabled her to love and serve without consideration for herself. Although the way the Spirit leads each person to respond to the love of the cross may look different, we are all under the same imperative: to love as Jesus loves. Like Mother Teresa, we decide how to respond to God's unique call to demonstrate this love in our lives.

As followers of Jesus who live by the Spirit, we are led to consistently serve and show kindness to people God brings into our lives. In doing so, we learn how deep and complicated each person is as we experience the rewards and pitfalls of sacrificial love. Unfortunately, the more we love, the more people expect us to love. Those who show great love usually receive intense disappointment when they fail. If done in our own strength, loving without expectation of return will burn us out. If we love immensely on occasion, yet are often intolerable or self-serving at other times, we will make little progress. Learning to love is the process of developing the stability and the fortitude to exhibit and share love wisely and consistently—in the Spirit's strength, not our own.

The difficulty of the call to love is acutely realized when confronted with a spouse, close friend, or relative who seems impossible to love. We may not want to risk the possibility of their criticizing us and taking advantage of our vulnerabilities. To a certain extent, when we have no emotional ties to people and can hide our weaknesses, we may find it easier to set our inhibitions aside and love with Christ's love. Yet the supernatural love of the Spirit enables us to stay engaged and show love even with those who are close and hard to love.

Teaching us to love as Jesus loves is the greatest miracle the Spirit can perform in our lives (1 Cor. 13:13). He actively moves us to have love for God, for one another, and for ourselves (1 John 2:15-17). Yet, the supernatural gift of love can be hard to handle. Like money, love can be used for beneficial or destructive causes. Love can be destructive if used to control, manipulate, or gain for oneself. Knowing this pitfall helps us understand why God does not instantly make all Christians miraculously loving. Until we are ready, we cannot sustain the cost and responsibility of love. Love is life's most precious and powerful commodity, yet it is one of the most challenging gifts to manifest selflessly with authenticity and consistency. If we are not first healed by the forgiveness and the love of Jesus, it may prove extremely difficult to handle such a great gift well.

The late president of Fuller Theological Seminary, Edward John Carnell, explained the complexities of love from a child's perspective in his book *The Kingdom of Love and the Pride of Life*, "That a person is good when he is kind and truthful."[36] Carnell points out that, like a child, we are to be quick to forgive, especially if the person had the right intentions.[37] He wrote about the principle of "double fulfillment" involved in love.[38] There are two ways to love: open and direct (being kind and truthful) and indirect (failing at love but attempting to love with the best intentions). When we fail, our struggle to learn to love is more important than legal perfection. Love can be difficult, but through the power of God's Spirit in us, we grow more loving. To be good and to be sanctified, we must become humble and see the world as a child does: making truth and love our highest priority and being quick to forgive and ask for forgiveness. These are the simple practices I see the Spirit leading me towards. Developing a childlike approach to love and forgiveness is key to enveloping our lives in God's love, allowing us to be a moldable block of clay God can shape into a beautiful and loving soul.

Whatever we do with our lives will be of lesser value if it is not done in God's love given by the Spirit. According to the Scriptures, we should have no shortage of love to give because the Father has lavished His love on us (1 John 3:1). There is nothing we can do to make God love us more, and there is nothing we can do to make God love us less. We have all His love, and it is not conditional on anything (Rom 8:38-39). The new covenant process of sanctification for the believer is learning to live in light of the love poured out in us (Rom. 5:5), and to share that love with ourselves and others. For "if we love one another, God resides in us, and his love is perfected in us" (First John 4:12, NET).

Chapter 23: Living A Good Life

I have been crucified with Christ, and it is no longer I who live, but Christ lives in me. So the life I now live in the body, I live because of the faithfulness of the Son of God, who loved me and gave himself for me.

Galatians 2:20 (NET)

CLAIMING JESUS CAME to provide a means to have a relationship with the Father, with His love perfected in us, is quite different from what some contend Jesus came for. If one claims Jesus came to change the world through improved government or social programs, they are not even close to understanding His objective. If someone contends He came to end hunger or eliminate sickness, there is little evidence to support that premise. Some might wish He came to end all war, but that didn't happen either. At least we might hope He came to alleviate suffering. Unfortunately, His disciples have endured great suffering over the centuries. However, none of the previous motives were His objective. Jesus came to take away the sin of the world, which provided a means to renew a loving relationship with Him and to create loving relationships with others and ourselves (John 1:29). In that endeavor, His success was far beyond measure—for through the cross, He not only took our sins away but He also taught us that love was more important than life itself.

It was also at the cross where the Father demonstrated that He intensely wanted a relationship with us, so much so, He was willing for His Son to suffer and die, that we should be called His children (1 John 3:1). Our adoption as His children and the Father's desire to lavish us with His great love is reckoned by Jesus' great sacrifice. His love will never be taken away because of our failures, and it does not increase when we follow the rules. When we receive Jesus' saving act of love on the cross, we enter and remain forever in a right relationship with God. In that restored relationship, bathed in complete forgiveness and filled with His life-giving Spirit, our transformation is realized (Rom. 5:5).

As I have demonstrated in previous chapters, even with the example of Christ's great loving sacrifice on the cross, and His command that we are to emulate that love as our experiential sanctification, many generations of Christians have still attempted to be sanctified by promoting a process of following laws and religious practices.

The church's role in sanctification has been misunderstood as well, being thought of as the source of blessings for good behavior and the corrector of bad behavior. It is hard for most to understand my teaching that promoting personal piety can have a negative effect on true sanctification, but it's true. Failing to realize that our transformation comes chiefly from loving as Jesus loved can lead to the opposite of love, which is expressed through the enforcement of legalistic practices. Deviation from the primacy of emulating the love of the cross has always led to religious work producing self-righteousness.

Human knowledge of good and evil has been the bane of mankind, used to judge others, ourselves, and even God. Still, it is highly apparent that humans need a source greater than themselves to define morality or our knowledge and definitions will become self-serving. Even though this is true, the definitions of right and wrong in human hands, religious or secular, quickly become a tool by which we judge and condemn others. As stated before, even Moses' law, which sought to teach us to love properly, devolved into a religion of judgment. Love becomes conditional under a religion of rules and reciprocity is required. This is not what God intended.

How do rules restrain the flesh? When we think of the flesh, we immediately think in terms of indulging ourselves in pleasure, comfort, and safety. Most of us don't recognize that restraining our sin with religion, personal efforts, and altruisms is living by the flesh as well. When we cross the line of indulging the flesh, we face condemnation and punishment. On the other hand, when we live the pious life of restraining the flesh, we appear holy, but unwanted fruits are still sprouting. Trusting our own power degrades our ability to love those who do not measure up and causes unmerited pride in our ability to follow the rules.

I cannot state this enough: practicing a form of Christianity where we become sanctified according to a list of rules is not Christ's plan. He sanctifies us by our faith in His truth and our practice of the sacrificial love of the cross (Phil. 3:9; Gal. 5:6). Jesus set aside the systems of rules, laws, obligations, and altruisms and replaced them all with one command: to love as He loves. Our practical sanctification is realized in our love for God, our treatment of our neighbors, and our respect for ourselves as we emulate the love of Jesus. This loving behavior can only be accomplished by God's Spirit guiding us in love and truth. We no longer follow rules to judge ourselves and others; instead, we seek and listen to the Spirit's guidance to love and do good and to not hate nor do evil.

Even those who agree Christians should live by grace and the guidance of the Spirit for their sanctification often find themselves thinking they still need both the law and the work of the cross to restrain the flesh. Living under both grace and the law is a distorted view of the new covenant. When we fail, we may find ourselves in a pattern of failure, guilt, confession, and perceived forgiveness. Those who participate in this formula fail to remove the old law and fail to put on the new garment of forgiveness and love that Jesus gives us.

Having grace and using it to follow the law is the act of sewing a new patch on an old garment (Matt. 2:21). This tear-and-repair lifestyle and ministry will trap a Christian into living by the flesh and not experiencing the fruits of the Spirit. Jesus gives us a new garment: a whole new way of life. When we are filled with God's Spirit, we should not use grace to help us live by the ministry of death (the law) or to repair our old garment of religious piety (2 Cor. 3:7). This only makes more holes. We need the new covenant of a life of love that Christ brings through His Spirit because we are no longer under the law of sin and death.

Jesus puts the Spirit's new wine of truth and love into new wineskins—our redeemed selves—vessels that will not burst. This is a life-freeing transformation. Despite this truth, it seems many Christians still attempt to put God's new wine into their old religious wineskin and then wonder why Jesus has not made a difference in their lives. In this scenario, our lives deteriorate with the same swiftness and severity as the non-believers because we still live by the world's rules. Individuals who point out that the work of the cross ended religious traditions are unwelcome. One cannot forcibly insert Jesus' new covenant into religion, and if they try, they may end up crucified like Christ. Sanctification by truth and love has no quarter with sanctification by rules; it is destined for an explosion. Jesus' new wine must be put into new wineskins, which will not burst (Matt 2:22).

This new wine in new wineskins is our source of sanctification from the inside out. Jesus said, "Nothing outside a person can defile them by going into them. Rather, it is what comes out of a person that defiles them" (Mark 7:15, NIV). This statement was upside-down to the Jews. How could Jesus say eating the wrong foods or touching an unclean item would not defile a person? His claim was against the law of Moses. Jesus reversed their interpretation of the rules by saying it was not what goes in but what comes out. According to the law, what someone ate or touched on the outside made them unclean. According to Jesus, if hate comes out, one is unclean; when love comes out, one is clean.

Jesus died on the cross to take away sin and fill us with His love, which made sin according to the law a non-issue for the believer (John 1:29). Still, as believers, we often ignore the Spirit, do evil and hateful actions, and fail to love. This is not who Jesus recreated us to be! We have the strength to walk in the light in His love. This is very different from living under a law that is powerless to accomplish love in us and often increases our sin. Jesus ended the curse of the law by becoming the curse for us (Gal. 3:13). The ministry of death, carved on stone as the Ten Commandments, no longer applies to us (2 Cor. 3:7). We have entered the ministry of life in Christ Jesus (Rom. 8:2).

The law of the Spirit, the new law written on our hearts, teaches us to love (Rom. 8:2). Every day, we fail to love in some capacity, and despite that, the Spirit continues to grow His love in us. The new law of the Spirit is a beautiful relationship. There is no condemnation; we simply learn from mistakes, leading to greater love. We are in a new covenant, following a new command: to love one another as He loved us and gave Himself up for us. Sanctification, by way of the cross, is living by the Spirit, empowering us to share unconditional and sacrificial love with everyone the Father brings into our lives.

Chapter 24: Things Not Included

Now the works of the flesh are obvious: sexual immorality, impurity, depravity, idolatry, sorcery, hostilities, strife, jealousy, outbursts of anger, selfish rivalries, dissensions, factions, envying, murder, drunkenness, carousing, and similar things. I am warning you, as I had warned you before: Those who practice such things will not inherit the kingdom of God! But the fruit of the Sprit is love, . . ."

Galatians 5:19-22 (NET)

ALTHOUGH ALL "WORKS of the flesh" are destructive and block our ability to love with the love of Christ, I will specifically address anger rooted in judgment to demonstrate how we are to live with the love of the cross. These are two self-evident indicators in our lives that something is not right. They both block love because their destructive natures directly attack another person. Loving a person while attacking them is almost impossible.

Anger is a major hindrance to love and spiritual growth in people. It is an uncontrollable monster. I have seen the most loving and beautiful people corrupted by fits of rage. I have witnessed anger as a way of life in my father and have struggled with it personally my whole life. At different times, I thought I had conquered anger and felt miserable when it got the best of me again.

Matthew recorded Jesus' words on anger:

> You have heard that it was said to our ancestors, Do not murder, and whoever murders will be subject to judgment. But I tell you, everyone who is angry with his brother will be subject to

judgment. And whoever says to his brother, 'Fool!' will be subject to the Sanhedrin. But whoever says, 'You moron!' will be subject to hellfire.

Matthew 5:21–22 (HCSB)

Jesus said that when we are angry at a person and call them stupid, it's a dumb thing for us to do, and we often suffer consequences. But, if our anger is such that we want a person to die and go to hell, and say it out loud, we are the ones in danger of hell.

How can Jesus connect anger to murder? Have you ever been mad enough to kill someone? The apostle John echoes Jesus, writing: "Everyone who hates his brother is a murderer" (1 John 3:15, NASB). Our judgment of those around us negatively engages our human emotions, sometimes even to the point of hate, which can possess us with the desire to destroy them. When we judge an offense we think was done with intent to harm, our anger steps in. Pastor Greg Boyd speaks the truth when he says, "When you judge, you cannot love."[39] Have you ever tried to love the object of your anger? Yet, we are called to love at all times. As believers, we are duplicitous and torn asunder when we are angry. Sometimes, when I am angry at the ones I love, I feel as if I am stretched over the fires of hell with my feet in hell and my hands grasping the eternal life that is in my heart and mind, or at least I thought it was. Nothing destroys my hope in salvation as much as anger. When Jesus says if I condemn someone in my anger, I am entering into the danger of hell; I agree with Him, for it tears me to pieces inside.

Having others know I struggle with anger invokes a tremendous fear for me as to what people think about it. Will they connect my anger to my father's abuse? Will they be repelled and want nothing to do with me ever again? Does it disqualify me from a position in ministry? Our current society sees the open display of anger as somewhat of an unforgivable sin.

My fear is not without substance, knowing the disturbing response a few people have had when they came to know the story of my father's abuse of my mother. They often assume that I am abusive because they think the son will repeat his father's behavior unless something extraordinary happens. Some are even bold enough, or perhaps thoughtless enough, to openly ask how I overcame this handicap, or they express amazement that I am not like my father.

To set the record straight, I am not abusive in any way like my father was. My story is different from his, and I was determined not to be like him regarding his abuse of my mother and his anger. I succeeded in many ways, except for my temper. That is not to say I could not easily have slipped into a life of abuse, but I chose not to succumb to any form of it. I have had God with me for my entire life, and I am convinced this was a big part of my saving grace.

Although I have had trouble controlling my anger at times, I can control my behavior when angry, which kept me out of a lot of trouble. Still, I hated my anger and became depressed when I lost my temper. No matter what I tried, it reared its ugly head. It was not until I realized the complete forgiveness and love Jesus provides, along with the understanding of the removal of the law, that I began to have control over my anger. As God taught me about freedom from sin and condemnation, and about the love He demonstrated to replace my rules, I could sense the Spirit taking away my propensity to judge. There was no rule by which I was condemned by God, so by what rule can I condemn and punish the objects of my anger? Was this not someone Jesus died for? How could I now curse them, especially if I am forgiven for all I have done?

How can I love someone when I am angry and judging them? My anger at people I perceive as wronging me is the opposite of love. Even if the person is a grave threat, if I were somehow able to love perfectly, I could allow them to destroy me for the sake of love. That's what Jesus did. When approaching others, there is nothing left for me to judge because Jesus has taken away their sins by taking them upon Himself. Could it be that judging and condemning others in my anger is equivalent to judging and condemning Jesus? Or, when I am angry at another believer, am I expressing anger at Jesus? My judgment and anger are contrary to living by the Spirit, preventing God's love from shining through me. He wants me to walk in love as He walked, knowing that He takes away the sin of the world, which should leave me with no reason to judge or be angry (John 17:26).

Many today may not relate to having angry responses to an offense, but I often see it in society. I have seen grown men get into a fistfight over a parking space. There was an unbelievable true story about a man who got so angry he shot a family member for taking a bite out of his grilled cheese sandwich.[40] Anger can put us in a state where we completely lose control of our ability to make reasoned decisions, be gracious, and love others. It is a debilitating emotion that can put a person in an uncontrollable state.

Although, at times, anger can be a misplaced emotion that covers fear and hurt, hides our weaknesses, or even reveals a chemical imbalance, most of the time, harmful anger is a reaction rooted in our judgment of other people's behaviors. When I am angry, I am in complete disagreement with another person's actions. I judge their actions as foolish or even judge them as fools and idiots who deserve my wrath. I find myself out of my mind that is taught by Christ to love.

Destructive judgment of others will quickly deteriorate any relationship. Looking at others with contempt changes our approach to them and sparks anger in the one who is judged. Judging others is the opposite of considering others better than ourselves (Phil. 2:3). Similarly, the degrading judgment of ourselves destroys our ability to love ourselves. Some even judge God, which prevents them from receiving His gift of love. This separation from Him happens entirely on our end, in our hearts and minds, for we know God does not stop loving us as His children even if we judge Him (Rom. 8:39). Being a judgmental person will darken our lives, preventing us from seeing His light and walking in it.

Jesus said, "Judge not, that you be not judged" (Matt. 7:1, NKJV). He admonished us to "first remove the plank from your own eye, and then you will see clearly to remove the speck that is in your brother's eye" (Luke 6:42, NKJV). Jesus warned us we would be judged by the same measure with which we judge others (Mark 4:24). He told us to "do to others as you would have them do to you" (Luke 6:31, NIV)—in other words, we should not negatively judge our neighbor since we don't want to be negatively judged.

The commandment not to judge can be confusing because it is normal for people to observe and judge behavior. We judge when we praise desired behavior and admire those with sound judgment. However, that is different from negative judgment of motives and offensive behaviors. We cannot live without some type of discerning judgment. We not only naturally judge our own behavior but also that of others. We constantly make judgments about truth, safety, efficiency, enjoyment, and how to love those around us. We function by judgment.

How can we not judge?

To answer this question, let us distinguish between two types of judgment: information input and negative judgment of another's behavior.

Information input includes observation, assessment, and movement or passivity.

1. Observation: We notice the things around us with our senses and make observations about our environment.
2. Assessment: We assess how the observed phenomena will affect us.
3. Movement or passivity: We decide whether to react or merely observe.

When Jesus said not to judge, He wasn't discussing information input. The judgment He spoke of concerned pointing out the sin or destruction of another and assigning motives.

Negative judgment of another's behavior includes observation, communication, and punishment.

1. Observing the "sin" or destructive behavior and possibly assigning motives.
2. Pointing out a person's negative behavior to them or others around them.
3. Exacting punishment for the behavior.

Everyone, including Jesus, observes negative behavior. Christians are not precluded from observing the effects of evil. So, the first one is a given and unavoidable. On the other hand, one might contend that unconditional love sometimes means trying our best not to notice offensive things, even though they may strain our senses. Too often, we make uninformed assumptions and judgments about the causes and motives of behavior. This may lead us to fail to empathize with the circumstances of the person who is doing the destruction. If evil intentions are not self-evident, assuming the best possible motive is the loving action to do.

Pointing out negative behavior can be tricky. We should not point out another's sin to a third party, which would be gossip and very unloving. Christians sometimes need to speak directly to the individual who is sinning, but this should be done in love and grace, not with law and judgment. We especially need the Spirit's guidance in these challenging situations, and we must keep the best interests of the person and those around them in mind.

Even with our purest intentions and best efforts, pointing out someone else's problem can go incredibly wrong. Sometimes, it is better to say nothing. The one place we are compelled as Christians to speak out is our obligation to tell people how to find life in Jesus. It is always more profitable to tell people about the love of Jesus than to judge their sins.

Christians should not be involved in exacting punishment from their brothers and sisters. Condemnation is up to God, the government, and others who are in a place of authority to carry out the work of judging on behalf of their appointed position. Even then, mercy is necessary and preferred. Leaders would be wise to remember the verse from the prophet Micah: "He has shown you, O man, what is good; And what does the Lord require of you; But to do justly, To love mercy, And to walk humbly with your God?" (Mic. 6:8, NKJV).

I struggle with judgment by leadership if it is legalistic and not based in love. In a recent spiritual leadership class, I was told it would be necessary to judge and discipline others as part of my leadership responsibilities in the church. The speaker was waxing on about how it was required as a leader to judge a church member and rebuke them for their sin. It all felt wrong to me. Should I go looking for people doing things wrong? Should my antenna always be up for something to correct? I could not keep silent. I informed him I would only correct someone in love. My correction would be based on what is the most loving thing to do for the person and others around them, and I would not judge people based on rules. I'm pretty sure I did not qualify for a leadership position in that church.

Unfortunately, our judgment is not limited to judging others. Often, we struggle with judging ourselves or telling ourselves destructive messages. We can go as far as self-condemnation and punishment. It's difficult to stop comparing, being jealous, and coveting. Only God's constant love can overcome judgment in our hearts, begin to perfect us in His love, and change how we think and act toward ourselves.

Even the world without Jesus can recognize that judgment hinders love, as the movie Shallow Hal demonstrates. In the story, Hal falls in love with a large, unattractive woman he thinks is skinny and beautiful because of a spell put on him. This is a woman he would have never liked if he were in a normal state of mind. When the spell is lifted, he must decide whether he loves her as she is. We can relate to Hal's dilemma because we are programmed to see the world as a place to meet our needs. However, in the movie we recognize the wrongness of that type of judgment. A needs-based view of the world forces us to judge others by whether they can fulfill our needs and desires. In Hal's world, it would mean finding someone who fits into certain beauty norms.

When God supplies all our needs, we are empowered to fill the needs of others, and we can trust Him to fill ours. He enables in us a giving approach to the world and removes our taking approach as we are perfected in cross-type love. God supplies us with what the world truly desires—the ability to see the person as who they are on the inside and not their outward appearance. "For the Lord does not see as man sees; for man looks at the outward appearance, but the Lord looks at the heart" (1 Sam. 16:7, NKJV). Shallow Hal, fortunately, ended up seeing past himself and saw the beautiful person he was dating. We can achieve the ability to see the world consistently and genuinely only by the supernatural presence of God's Spirit in us, which enables us to live with the love of the cross.

As God perfects us in the love of the cross, His Spirit will daily—and even moment by moment—instruct us in His love. Anger and judgment are definite signs something is wrong. However, like all evil, focusing on it will not eliminate it. We overcome the flesh by living in God's love, by the power of His Spirit. Overcoming anger and judgment are the two areas the Spirit has laid heavy on my heart in teaching me to love. Your weakness may not be the same as mine because God made each one of us different. As the Spirit teaches us to love more each day, He will continue to build us up, help us overcome our weaknesses, and grow us to love with sacrificial love. We must walk in His light with our minds focused on loving as Jesus loved and seek His help to overcome the works of the flesh.

Chapter 25: Love-Side-Up

Beloved, if God so loved us, we also ought to love one another ...if we love one another, God abides in us, and His love is perfected in us.

First John 4:11–12 (NASB)

IN ORDER TO BRING US the *good life,* the infinite God of love invaded the kingdom of man, not to take it over and set up a new earthly kingdom, instead, to demonstrate perfect love by dying on a cross to reconcile humanity to Himself (2 Cor. 5:19). The throne of His new kingdom was not the Throne of David, nor a throne of conquest, but was the humiliation of the cross, portraying a kingdom of unconditional love and sacrifice (1 Cor. 1:23). It is also not a kingdom brought on by might or power but a kingdom that will be realized by His Spirit pouring out His love in our hearts (Rom. 5:5). This is a kingdom in which we know and love God, and He knows and loves us. In a similar way, we strive to know and love one another and ourselves. Living for God's kingdom will turn our lives *love-side-up.*

As we seek God's new heavenly kingdom of love in our lives and embrace our new King, we will find earthly purposes for our lives that work hand in hand with His heavenly purpose, and our self-serving kingdom begins to fade as a priority (Matt. 6:33). This transformation begins when we embrace and experience a higher kingdom of reconciliation with God, learn the truth of our salvation, and learn to emulate the love Jesus demonstrated on the cross. God's kingdom of love is not a kingdom of power and success in the world's eyes; it is a kingdom where success is akin to sacrifice, and status is defined as the least being the greatest. The world would label our new priorities as backward or upside-down, but I like to say that the love of the cross turns our lives *love-side-up*.

The gospel is what makes our entrance into God's kingdom possible. The essence of the gospel is not that we are sinners in need of forgiveness, for our sin is not "good news," and salvation is not merely the forgiveness of sins. The gospel is the good news that God loves us, desires to restore a relationship with us, and He joined His creation and suffered on the cross for that potential relationship—taking away our sin and guilt so we can return to His family. We enter God's family when we choose to believe and follow Jesus as God, the giver of life, and we understand that out of His love for us, He died in our place and rose from the dead. The cross and the resurrection demonstrated His power over sin and death, and His desire to give us eternal life. Eternal life means you, as a person, will exist forever with Jesus, where He dwells. We currently have a down payment of this eternal life through the Holy Spirit indwelling in us, and we will be taken to be with Jesus when we die (2 Cor. 5:1-5). All this is made possible through the Son's sacrifice, which resolved our state of destruction and separation from God. Anyone who decides to believe in and follow Jesus as God is declared righteous, which makes them worthy to be indwelt by the Holy Spirit as a guide and comforter. Our Spirit-filled transformation takes place immediately upon our belief and is not something that happens when we die—for, in the very moment we believe, we receive the Holy Spirit.

The cross and the Spirit in us change the paradigm of our sanctification as believers. Rather than follow the law of Moses, or any other religious rule or practice as the means to be sanctified, we follow the Spirit who teaches us to love with sacrificial love, which is true goodness. There are many sources the Spirit can use to guide us, including the Bible, the church, and other Christians. In addition, He guides our thoughts, speech, and actions if we are able to listen. Jesus did not intend life to be lived with a list of what we should and should not do, constantly judging ourselves and our neighbors; He intended it to be a life of love and relationship with Him and others, guided by the Spirit and the love He demonstrated for us.

We now live this life differently in light of the eternity we have entered. We walk this journey with the Holy Spirit directing and comforting us, and we aspire to live the love Jesus demonstrated on the cross, joined with the very brothers and sisters with whom we will spend eternity. The good that we practice and the loving person we become here are a large portion of who we will be in heaven. But if we practice hate, and there is no hate allowed in heaven, how much of our earthly selves will be in heaven with God when we get there (1 Cor. 3:15)? Will it be merely a shell of who we are now in the flesh, or will it be the loving person that we have become in Christ? How we grow in knowing the truth of our salvation and demonstrating His love forms us and changes us into God's new creation that we will be in heaven.

Our new life of love is experienced through living by what Paul calls the "law of the Spirit" (Rom. 8:2, NIV). We are completely forgiven, with no condemnation, and without the law of sin and death enslaving us. Knowing there is no condition in which God will take His love from us frees us to openly admit and work on any fault we have. We are free to make any decision we want at any given point. We are not tethered by past failures, rules, obligations, guilt, or condemnation heaped upon us. We are also not hindered by a fear of future mistakes. We are entirely free and empowered to do the best, right, loving action, and we are instructed on how to do this as the Spirit leads us in His love.

To further experience this new freedom in Christ, the apostle Paul admonishes us to "not be conformed to this world, but be transformed by the renewing of your mind, so that you may prove what the will of God is, that which is good and acceptable and perfect" (Rom. 12:2, NASB). John says for us "not [to] love the world nor the things in the world. If anyone loves the world, the love of the Father is not in him" (1 John 2:15, NASB). Jesus wants to free us from the world's ways of manipulation and the threat we once used to serve ourselves as a means to retain our relationships, wealth, power, safety, and comfort. God has given us a whole new way to live. It is not a self-help system or a list of rules to avoid sin, rather it is a life that can only be lived consistently by the truth, love, and hope we receive from the Holy Spirit.

This new mindset God gives us is an entirely different way of thinking and a completely different way of approaching life. As we discard the world's vision of success and replace it with Jesus' forgiveness and love as the center focus of our lives, our worldview changes. We leave the way of violence and enter the way of love; we leave the way of excessive grief and enter the way of comfort; we leave the way of hoarding money and enter the way of charity;

we leave the way of desperately seeking safety and comfort and enter a life of willingness to embrace suffering; we leave the way of seeking validation and acceptance and embrace the way of potential rejection; we leave the way of the familiar and embark on a life of the unknown. Instead of the way of the world, we travel the way of the Spirit. Jesus said, "The wind blows wherever it pleases. You hear its sound, but you cannot tell where it comes from or where it is going. So it is with everyone born of the Spirit" (John 3:8, NIV). The world does not know who our Father is, nor understand the love of the Son, nor receive the guidance of the Spirit, so they cannot understand, predict, or control what we do and where we go on this journey. This change can be terrifying for those who prefer to be in control. When we follow Jesus, we enter the unpredictable way of the cross.

The way of the cross, the way of sacrificial love as we walk with the Spirit, is spurred on by our understanding of the humility and sacrifice Jesus made. Knowing how much Jesus loves each person and that He died a brutal death for all is a key to preparing our minds to love and forgive each individual we meet. This is a love that humbly thinks of others first and strives for their safety and wellbeing. We see each person as important because they are someone Jesus loved. Unfortunately, merely knowing His love will not make us into a loving person. It is still only by the Spirit's power in us that we can embody unending, sacrificial, and unconditional love for our neighbors and even for ourselves.

The Spirit not only enables us to love, He perfects the Love of Jesus in us. John conveyed this when he wrote:

> Whoever confesses that Jesus is the Son of God, God abides in him, and he in God. We have come to know and have believed the love which God has for us. God is love, and the one who abides in love abides in God, and God abides in him. By this, love is perfected with us, so that we may have confidence in the day of judgment; because as He is, so also are we in this world. There is no fear in love; but perfect love casts out fear, because fear involves punishment, and the one who fears is not perfected in love. We love, because He first loved us.

First John 4:15–19 (NASB)

The one who understands that sanctification in the Christian life is about perfecting the love of Jesus in us is the one who lives in peace, filled with God, and without fear of punishment. When we live our lives dominated by His love, God begins to melt away our past in His complete forgiveness. In His love we are free to become someone our past says we are not and someone our negativity says we cannot be in the future. There is little limit on the life transformation we can aspire to when bathed in God's love and living by the power of His Spirit.

Unfortunately, being perfected in His love does not take away our suffering––it is more of a way to endure it. Sacrifice, struggle, and suffering are what Christ demonstrated on the cross in His great act to unconditionally love us. We should not avoid living out the suffering of the cross because following Jesus means being willing to embrace hardship for the sake of love. In the power of the Spirit, we are to live with the love of the cross towards others, whatever that demands.

Even in our distress, it is important to know that God is always on our side. He does not condemn us with struggle, instead He joins us as we walk this tumultuous and yet eventful life. Jesus loves us and moves us toward truth and love so we can experience this *good life* as He intended. He wants us to embrace life, with all its turns and twists, as we struggle together with the Holy Spirit by our side, experiencing all life has to offer. We thrive with Him, learning to deeply love and care for ourselves and the people around us, while participating in all the fantastic adventures God has in store for us.

Our salvation is freedom, and God wants to give us an amazingly *good life* in light of our new outlook! This life is freedom from the bondage of sin and freedom from religion as well. We are set free from the old covenant of living under the condemnation of law and judgment, and we enter the new covenant of a life of glory in the Spirit. The Spirit is transforming us into the image of the Lord. Paul wrote concerning this transformation:

> But when one turns to the Lord, the veil is removed. Now the Lord is the Spirit, and where the Spirit of the Lord is present, there is freedom. And we all, with unveiled faces reflecting the glory of

the Lord, are being transformed into the same image from one degree of glory to another, which is from the Lord, who is the Spirit.

Second Corinthians 3:16-18 (NET)

Our new freedom in His forgiveness and love, along with the Spirit transforming us to love with Christ's love, brings a new glory to our lives. We are now growing and reflecting God's glory.

Salvation provides not only promises of our glory here in this life, but also the knowledge that our future will bring great comfort. John professed he heard the angels proclaim:

> God's dwelling place is now among the people, and he will dwell with them. They will be his people, and God himself will be with them and be their God. 'He will wipe every tear from their eyes. There will be no more death' or mourning or crying or pain, for the old order of things has passed away.

Revelation 21:3–4 (NIV)

The promise of the next life is good for those who follow Jesus!

As a follower of Jesus, we do not have to do anything for our salvation but will want to do everything we can to live out His love. His Spirit dwelling in us will transform our lives if we let Him. When we believed in the Lord Jesus, we were saved, and the love of the cross—lived by the power of the Spirit––began to transform our existence and open a whole new, abundant life for us to live. He brings this *good life* profoundly present in our lives. God's love pours out into our hearts when we become His children, and nothing can separate us from His love (Rom. 5:5, 8:38-39). We can do nothing to make God love us more, and we can do nothing to make God love us less. Sin between God and us is no more, and it is replaced by His love. We have all His love, and it is not conditional on anything. With that kind of love behind us, in us, and before us, we are left with no other viable option but to walk in His deep love for us. His great love for us does not turn our world upside-down; it turns our lives *love-side-up* by resurrecting the cross in our life, empowering us to live the *good life* of being perfected in His love.

BIBLIOGRAPHY

Arlandson, James M., *Historical Reliability of the Gospels. Did Some Disciples Take Notes During Jesus' Ministry?* Bible.org, 2020. https://bible.org/seriespage/8-did-some-disciples-take-notes-during-jesus-ministry.

Baukham, *Richard, Jesus and the Eyewitnesses: The Gospels as Eyewitness Testimony.* Second ed., Grand Rapids: Eerdmans, 2017, Summary given by Robert J Cara, *Reformed Faith & Practice*. https://journal.rts.edu/review/jesus-and-the-eyewitnesses-the-gospels-as-eyewitness-testimony/.

Boyd, Greg, *Sociopath Religion*. The Narrow Gate, July 3, 2013. https://youtu.be/-3sZr8IWbKs.

Britannica.com

Bromiley, Geoffrey W., *The International Standard Bible Encyclopedia, Vol. 4, Q-Z*. Grand Rapids, Eerdmans, 1988.

Budjen, Aaron, 2020. www.livinggodministries.net[1].

Budjen, Aaron, *Hebrews 6:1 Dead Works, Hebrews Message*. Living God Ministries website, https://www.livinggodministries.net/living_god_ministries/radio_archive/audio_files/hebrews_20_ch6_1_dead_works.mp3.

Budjen, Aaron, *Cloth and Wine*. Living God Ministries. https://www.livinggodministries.net/living_god_ministries/radio_archive/audio_files/cloth_and_wine.mp3

Burridge, Richard, *What are the Gospels?* 1992/2004. http://www.fondazioneratzinger.va/content/fondazioneratzinger/en/news/notizie/rimandi-news/graeco-roman-biography-and-the-gospels-literary-genre.html.

Carnell, Edward John, *The Kingdom of Love and the Pride of Life*. Grand Rapids, Wm. B. Eerdmans, 1960.

The Church of Jesus Christ of the Latter Day Saints, *Attributes of Christ*. https://www.churchofjesuschrist.org/comeuntochrist/believe/becoming-like-jesus/attributes-of-christ.

Crossway, *The Bible and Islam*. https://www.crossway.org/articles/the-bible-and-islam/.

Farley, Andrew, *God Without Religion*. Grand Rapids, Baker Books, 2011.

Fusselman, *Midge, What Blaise Pascal Saw In A November Night of Fire That Inaugurated A Year Of Grace*. The Federalist, 2020. https://thefederalist.com/2017/11/23/blaise-pascal-saw-november-night-fire-inaugurated-year-grace/.

Holloway, April. *Accounts of Roman Infanticide and Sacrifice All Just Myth and Legend?* Ancient Origins, September 5, 2015. https://www.ancient-origins.net/news-history-archaeology/accounts-roman-infanticide-and-sacrifice-all-just-myth-and-legend-006591.

Instone-Brewer, David, *Jesus of Nazareth's Trial in the Uncensored Talmud*. Tyndale Bulletin 62.2, 2011. http://legacy.tyndale.cam.ac.uk/Tyndale/staff/Instone-Brewer/prepub/07_Instone_Brewer.pdf.

Klein, Christopher, *The Bible Says Jesus Was Real, What Other Proof Exists?* history.com, April 16, 2019. https://www.history.com/news/was-jesus-real-historical-evidence.

Liddel-Scott-Jones Definitions, Entry for Strong's #863, Studylight.org, 2020. https://www.studylight.org/lexicons/greek/863.html.

Liddel-Scott-Jones Definitions, Entry for Strong's #2511, Studylight.org, 2020. https://www.studylight.org/lexicons/greek/2511.html.

Liddel-Scott-Jones Definitions, Entry for Strong's #93, Studylight.org, 2020. https://www.studylight.org/lexicons/greek/93.html.

Marrow, Johnathan, *Helping a New Generation Build a Lasting Faith: What Did the Jewish Historian Josephus Say About Jesus?* 2020. https://www.jonathanmorrow.org/?s=early+roman+documents+about+Jesus&sub

The Metropolitan Museum of Art, *The Five Pillars of Islam*. https://www.metmuseum.org/learn/educators/curriculum-resources/art-of-the-islamic-world/unit-one/the-five-pillars-of-islam.

Musumeci, Natalie, *Man Shoots at wife and daughter over grilled cheese sandwich: cops*. New York Post, nypost.com, January 9, 2017. https://nypost.com/2017/01/09/man-shoots-at-wife-and-daughter-over-grilled-cheese-sandwich-cops/.

Newsroom, *What Mormons Believe About Jesus Christ*. Church of Jesus Christ and Latter Day Saints. https://newsroom.churchofjesuschrist.org/article/what-mormons-believe-about-jesus-christ.

Oxford English Dictionary, 2020. https://www.oed.com/viewdictionaryentry/Entry/110566.

Pascal, Blaise, *Pensées*, trans. Honor Levi (Oxford: Oxford University Press,1995.

Popova, Maria, *What Is Love? Famous Definitions from 400 Years of Literary History,"* May 28th, 2020. https://www.brainpickings.org/2013/01/01/what-is-love/.

Reeves, Ryan M., PhD Cambridge, *Martin Luther and Antinomianism, Church History: Reformation to Modern*, March 2, 2015. https://youtu.be/f44SbUJuWd4?si=310GMaDy72HlSsJx.

Rivera, John, *The historical Jesus and the Bible Scholars cast doubt on miracles, Easter.* The Baltimore Sun, September 7, 2020. https://www.baltimoresun.com/news/bs-xpm-1998-05-03-1998123040-story.html.

Ryle, J. C., *The Cross*. First Edition 1852, pg. 26, Abbottsford, Aneko Press, Revised Edition, 2019.

Sanders, John, *The Perennial Debate*. Christianity Today, Christianity Today International, 14 May 1990.

Stanley, Andy, *Irresistible: Reclaiming the New that Jesus Unleashed for the World*. Grand Rapids, Zondervan, 2018.

Strong's Concordance. BibleHub.com.
https://www.Biblehub.com/greek/266.htm.

Studylight.org

Thiede, Carsten Peter, *A Testament Is Born*. Christian History Institute, Issue #43, 1994.
https://christianhistoryinstitute.org/magazine/article/a-testament-is-born.

Wallace, J. Warner, *Good Reasons to Believe Peter Is the Source of Mark's Gospel*. Cold Case Christianity. August 24th, 2018.
https://coldcasechristianity.com/writings/good-reasons-to-believe-peter-is-the-source-of-marks-gospel/.

Zacharias, Ravi, *How can we show that Christianity is the true religion*? Ravi Zacharias International Ministries, April 2, 2012.
https://www.youtube.com/watch?v=nWY-6xBA0Pk&feature=youtu.be.

ENDNOTES

[1] Pascal, Blaise, *Pensées*, pp. 63–64, trans. Honor Levi. Oxford: Oxford University Press, 1995.

[2] Morrow, Jonathan. "What Did the Jewish Historian Josephus Really Say about Jesus?" Jonathan Morrow, November 4, 2016. https://www.jonathanmorrow.org/what-did-the-jewish-historian-josephus-really-say-about-jesus/ .

[3] Klein, Christopher, "The Bible Says Jesus Was Real. What Other Proof Exists?" history.com, April 16, 2019, https://www.history.com/news/was-jesus-real-historical-evidence .

[4] Klein, Christopher, "The Bible Says Jesus Was Real. What Other Proof Exists?" history.com, April 16, 2019, https://www.history.com/news/was-jesus-real-historical-evidence .

[5] Instone-Brewer, David, "Jesus of Nazareth's Trial in the Uncensored Talmud, page 275, Tyndale Bulletin 62.2, 2011, http://legacy.tyndale.cam.ac.uk/Tyndale/staff/Instone-Brewer/prepub/07_Instone_Brewer.pdf .

[6] Instone-Brewer, David, "Jesus of Nazareth's Trial in the Uncensored Talmud, page 275, Tyndale Bulletin 62.2, 2011, http://legacy.tyndale.cam.ac.uk/Tyndale/staff/Instone-Brewer/prepub/07_Instone_Brewer.pdf .

[7] Sanders, John. "The Perennial Debate." ChristianityToday.com. Christianity Today, April 1, 2000. https://www.christianitytoday.com/ct/2000/aprilweb-only/12.0a.html .

[8] Aaron Budjen, www.livinggodministries.net[1] , 2020.

[9] "Strong's #2588 - Καρδία - Old & New Testament Greek Lexical Dictionary." StudyLight.org, n.d. https://www.studylight.org/lexicons/eng/greek/2588.html .

[10] "Strong's #5590 - Ψυχή - Old & New Testament Greek Lexical Dictionary." StudyLight.org, n.d. https://www.studylight.org/lexicons/eng/greek/5590.html .

[11] "Strong's #1271 - Διάνοια - Old & New Testament Greek Lexical Dictionary." StudyLight.org, n.d. https://www.studylight.org/lexicons/eng/greek/1271.html .

[12] "Strong's #2479 - Ἰσχύς - Old & New Testament Greek Lexical Dictionary." StudyLight.org, n.d. https://www.studylight.org/lexicons/eng/greek/2479.html .

---

1. http://www.livinggodministries.net

[13] Fusselman, Midge. "What Blaise Pascal Saw in a November Night of Fire." The Federalist, November 23, 2017. https://thefederalist.com/2017/11/23/blaise-pascal-saw-november-night-fire-inaugurated-year-grace/ .

[14] Ryle, J. C., *The Cross*, First Edition 1852, Abbotsford, Aneko Press, Revised Edition, 2019, Pg, 26.

[15] Bromiley, Geoffrey W., *The International Standard Bible Encyclopedia*, Vol. 4, Q-Z, Pg, 193, Eerdmans, 1988.

[16] Bromiley, Geoffrey W., *The International Standard Bible Encyclopedia*, Vol. 4, Q-Z, Pg,193, Eerdmans, 1988.

[17] Bromiley, Geoffrey W., *The International Standard Bible Encyclopedia*, Vol. 4, Q-Z, Pg,193, Eerdmans, 1988.

[18] Bromiley, Geoffrey W., *The International Standard Bible Encyclopedia*, Vol. 4, Q-Z, Pg,193, Eerdmans, 1988.

[19] Bromiley, Geoffrey W., *The International Standard Bible Encyclopedia*, Vol. 4, Q-Z, Pg,193, Eerdmans, 1988.

[20] Stanley, Andy, Irresistible: Reclaiming the New that Jesus Unleashed for the World, pg. 196, Zondervan, Grand Rapids, 2018.

[21] Farley, Andrew, God Without Religion, book summary, Baker Books, Grand Rapids, 2011.

[22] Budjen, Aaron, "Hebrews 6:1 Dead Works," Hebrews Message, Living God Ministries website. https://www.livinggodministries.net/living_god_ministries/radio_archive/audio_files/hebrews_20_ch6_1_dead_works.mp3 .

[23] Reeves, Ryan M., PhD Cambridge, "Martin Luther and Antinomianism," Church History: Reformation to Modern, March 2, 2015, https://youtu.be/f44SbUJuWd4?si=310GMaDy72HlSsJx .

[24] Reeves, Ryan, Ibid.

[25] Unknown, quoted on KLOVE by announcer, June 2020.

[26] "Evagrius Ponticus," The Editors of Encyclopedia Britannica, Britannica.com. January 1, 2022. https://www.britannica.com/biography/Evagrius-Ponticus.

[27] "Seven Deadly Sins," The Editors of Encyclopedia Britannica, Britannica.com. January 1, 2022. https://www.britannica.com/topic/seven-deadly-sins .

[28] "Strong's Greek: 266. Ἁμαρτία (Hamartia)." BibleHub, n.d. https://www.Biblehub.com/greek/266.htm .

[29] Budjen, Aaron, "Cloth and Wine," Living God Ministries. https://www.livinggodministries.net/living_god_ministries/radio_archive/audio_files/cloth_and_wine.mp3 .

[30] "Strong's #2511 - Καθαρίζω - Old & New Testament Greek Lexical Dictionary." StudyLight.org, n.d. https://www.studylight.org/lexicons/greek/2511.html .

[31] "Strong's #93 - Ἀδικία - Old & New Testament Greek Lexical Dictionary." StudyLight.org, n.d. https://www.studylight.org/lexicons/greek/93.html .

[32] Oxford English Dictionary, 2020. https://www.oed.com/viewdictionaryentry/Entry/110566[2] .

[33] Popova, Maria, "What Is Love? Famous Definitions from 400 Years of Literary History," May 28th, 2020, https://www.brainpickings.org/2013/01/01/what-is-love/ .

[34] Popova, Maria, "What Is Love? Famous Definitions from 400 Years of Literary History," May 28th, 2020, https://www.brainpickings.org/2013/01/01/what-is-love/ .

[35] Boyd, Greg, "Sociopath Religion." The Narrow Gate. July 3, 2013. https://youtu.be/-3sZr8IWbKs .

[36] Carnell, Edward John, *The Kingdom of Love and the Pride of Life*. Grand Rapids, Michigan: Wm. B. Eerdmans, 1960, p. 17.

[37] Carnell, Edward John, *The Kingdom of Love and the Pride of Life*. Grand Rapids, Michigan: Wm. B. Eerdmans, 1960, p. 130.

[38] Carnell, Edward John, *The Kingdom of Love and the Pride of Life*. Grand Rapids, Michigan: Wm. B. Eerdmans, 1960, p. 130.

[39] Boyd, Greg, "Sociopath Religion." The Narrow Gate. June 3, 2013. https://youtu.be/-3sZr8IWbKs .

[40] Musumeci, Natalie, "Man Shoots at Wife and Daughter Over Grilled Cheese Sandwich: Cops." January 9, 2017. New York Post, nypost.com. https://nypost.com/2017/01/09/man-shoots-at-wife-and-daughter-over-grilled-cheese-sandwich-cops/ .

---

2. https://www.oed.com/viewdictionaryentry/Entry/110566.%5C

About the Author

Ernest Randolph has been in ministry since 1986, working with youth and adults, pointing them to Jesus. After graduating with his master's in Youth Ministry from Denver Seminary in 1994, he worked as a youth pastor, as well as a lay pastor in churches around the Denver area. For the last few years, he has followed a call to lead a Bible study in the local bar, teaching the Word of God to a whole new demographic. This opportunity has forced him to dig deep into the biblical message of salvation and discover how God has provided the perfect means to save everyone: rich, poor, strong, weak, young, old, sinner, or saint. The way of the cross kept screaming out to him as the only way possible to provide for the reconciling of all people from all walks of life to God. He wrote this book to remind you of that same message of the cross, which is the life-changing power of God to everyone who believes.

Read more at https://lovesideup.org/.

www.ingramcontent.com/pod-product-compliance
Lightning Source LLC
Chambersburg PA
CBHW060822050426
42453CB00008B/550